W9-AMB-700

1940–1960

The Twentieth Century

**Other books in the
Events That Changed the World series:**

EVENTS THAT CHANGED THE WORLD

1940–1960

═ The Twentieth Century ═

Jennifer A. Bussey, *Book Editor*

Daniel Leone, *President*
Bonnie Szumski, *Publisher*
Scott Barbour, *Managing Editor*

GREENHAVEN
PRESS ®

THOMSON
—————★—————™
GALE

San Diego • Detroit • New York • San Francisco • Cleveland
New Haven, Conn. • Waterville, Maine • London • Munich

For more information, contact
Greenhaven Press
27500 Drake Rd.
Farmington Hills, MI 48331-3535
Or you can visit our Internet site at http://www.gale.com

Cover credit: © Bettmann/CORBIS
Library of Congress, 21, 104, 144
National Archives, 30, 47
U.S. Navy, 80

LIBRARY OF CONGRESS CATALOGING-IN-PUBLICATION DATA

1940–1960 / Jennifer A. Bussey, book editor.
  p. cm. — (Events that changed the world)
Includes bibliographical references and index.
ISBN 0-7377-1757-2 (pbk. : alk. paper) —
ISBN 0-7377-1756-4 (lib. bdg. : alk. paper)
  1. World War, 1939–1945. 2. Cold War. 3. Revolutions—China. 4. United
States—Social life and customs—1945–1970. 5. World politics—1945–1955.
I. Bussey, Jennifer A. II. Series.
D743.A14 2004
909.82'4—dc21   2002192798

CONTENTS

number of dead, and the state of the survivors all told a horrifying story.

Event 5: The Bombing of Hiroshima and Nagasaki: August 6 and 9, 1945

1. Hiroshima and Nagasaki Ushered in the Atomic Age

by Rinjiro Sodei

The bomb was a major factor in Japan's surrender, which ended World War II. The event also launched decades of suffering for the survivors and initiated the nuclear age. Historians continue to grapple with its consequences.

2. Defending the Use of the Atomic Bomb

by Winston S. Churchill

After warning Japan to surrender, the Allies had no choice but to use the atomic bomb to bring a swift end to the war. Though destructive, the bomb brought peace.

Event 6: The Nuremberg Trials: November 20, 1945–August 31, 1946

1. The Nuremberg Trials Ushered in a New International Legal Code

by William J. Bosch

The discovery of the Nazi's atrocities compelled the Allies to form an international tribunal to try Nazi leaders for their war crimes. This history-making court proved that wartime conduct carried serious consequences.

2. Excerpts from the Nuremberg Trial Transcripts

During private meetings, Hitler and other top Nazi officials made plans to kill large groups of people for reasons of ethnicity, inferiority, and political views. They also used camp prisoners to carry out dangerous missions.

Event 9: The People's Republic of China Is Established: October 1, 1949

Event 10: Rosa Parks Refuses to Surrender Her Bus Seat: December 1, 1955

Event 11: Elvis "the King of Rock and Roll" Presley Signs with RCA: December 1955

Event 12: The Soviets Launch *Sputnik*: October 4, 1957

FOREWORD

In 1543 a Polish astronomer named Nicolaus Copernicus published a book entitled *De revolutionibus orbium coelestium* in which he theorized that Earth revolved around the Sun. In 1688, during the Glorious Revolution, Dutch prince William of Orange invaded England and overthrew King James II. In 1922 Irish author James Joyce's novel *Ulysses*, which describes one day in Dublin, was published.

Although these events are seemingly unrelated, occurring in different nations and in different centuries, they all share the distinction of having changed the world. Although Copernicus's book had a relatively minor impact at the time of its publication, it eventually had a momentous influence. The Copernican system provided a foundation on which future scientists could develop an accurate understanding of the solar system. Perhaps more importantly, it required humanity to contemplate the possibility that Earth, far from occupying a special place at the center of creation, was merely one planet in a vast universe. In doing so, it forced a reevaluation of the Christian cosmology that had served as the foundation of Western culture. As professor Thomas S. Kuhn writes, "The drama of Christian life and the morality that had been made dependent upon it would not readily adapt to a universe in which the earth was just one of a number of planets."

Like the Copernican revolution, the Glorious Revolution of 1688–1689 had a profound influence on the future of Western societies. By deposing James II, William and his wife, Mary, ended the Stuart dynasty, a series of monarchs who had favored the Catholic Church and had limited the power of Parliament for decades. Under William and Mary, Parliament passed the Bill of Rights, which established the legislative supremacy of Parliament and barred Roman Catholics from the throne. These actions initiated the gradual process by which the power of the government of England shifted from the monarchy to Parliament, establishing a democratic system that would be copied, with some variations, by the United States and other democratic societies worldwide.

Whereas the Glorious Revolution had a major impact in the political sphere, the publication of Joyce's novel *Ulysses* represented a revolution in literature. In an effort to capture the sense of chaos and discontinuity that permeated the culture in the wake of World War I, Joyce did away with the use of straightforward narrative that had dominated fiction up to that time. The novel, whose structure mirrors that of Homer's *Odyssey*, combines realistic descriptions of events with passages that convey the characters' inner experience by means of a technique known as stream of consciousness, in which the characters' thoughts and feelings are presented without regard to logic or narrative order. Due to its departure from the traditional modes of fiction, *Ulysses* is often described as one of the seminal works of modernist literature. As stated by Pennsylvania State University professor Michael H. Begnal, "*Ulysses* is the novel that changed the direction of 20th-century fiction written in English."

Copernicus's theory of a sun-centered solar system, the Glorious Revolution, and James Joyce's *Ulysses* are just three examples of time-bound events that have had far-reaching effects—for better or worse—on the progress of human societies worldwide. History is made up of an inexhaustible list of such events. In the twentieth century alone, for example, one can isolate any number of world-shattering moments: the first performance of Igor Stravinsky's ballet *The Rites of Spring* in 1913; Japan's attack on Pearl Harbor on December 7, 1941; the launch of the satellite *Sputnik* on October 4, 1957. These events variously influenced the culture, society, and political configuration of the twentieth century.

Greenhaven Press's Events That Changed the World series is designed to help readers learn about world history by examining seemingly random events that have had the greatest influence on the development of cultures, societies, and governments throughout the ages. The series is divided into sets of several anthologies, with each set covering a period of one hundred years. Each volume begins with an introduction that provides essential context on the time period being covered. Then, the major events of the era are covered by means of primary and secondary sources. Primary sources include firsthand accounts, speeches, correspondence, and other materials that bring history alive. Secondary sources analyze the profound effects the events had on the world. Each reading is preceded by an introduction that puts it in context and emphasizes the event's importance in the ongoing evolution of world history. Additional features add to the value of the series: An annotated table of contents and an index allow readers to quickly locate material of interest. A chronology provides an easy reference for contextual information. And a bibliography offers opportunities for further exploration. All of these features help to make the Events That Changed the World series a valuable resource for readers interested in the major events that have shaped the course of humanity.

INTRODUCTION

The dynamic and eventful years between 1940 and 1960 are underscored by events of unprecedented worldwide impact. Critical chapters in world history unfolded during this time that left the world a very different place. From the rising sun of Japan to the rising star of Elvis Presley, politics, music, international affairs, civil rights, and science were transformed during these two decades. Whereas some of these events revealed the very worst tendencies of humanity, others are among humanity's finest moments.

World War II shattered the entire world's sense of security. People all over the world—leaders and citizens alike—realized that World War I was not the "war to end all wars." In the United States, the Japanese surprise attack on Pearl Harbor in 1941 forced Americans to heighten their sense of vulnerability. Americans realized that they were not immune to the terrors of war.

As World War II raged on, Americans were scared, and policies began to reflect that fear. President Franklin D. Roosevelt ordered that Japanese Americans report to internment camps. Fear and uncertainty about Japanese spies prompted many Americans to overcome their pride in individual rights to take away the rights of other Americans. In the 1950s, the Senator Joseph McCarthy Communist hearings allowed for a similar debacle. The "red scare" became a modern-day witch-hunt in which alleged Communists were ostracized socially and politically. Careers, lives, and families were destroyed.

Toward the end of World War II, Allied troops began to liberate Nazi concentration camps, and the world came to recognize the unprecedented inhumanity Adolf Hitler had directed at people he considered undesirable, primarily Jews. These discoveries sent waves of sadness, horror, and rage across the globe. Americans and Russians were aghast to learn how diabolical their enemy had actually been, and most Europeans were simultaneously devastated that such a thing had happened in their own backyards and relieved that a monster like Hitler was no longer in power. The tensions in Europe between Germans and other nationalities created deep rifts on personal and political levels.

The dropping of the atomic bombs on Hiroshima and Nagasaki claimed well over one hundred thousand civilian lives. Such a weapon had been unimaginable until its full destructive power was unleashed at the end of World War II. Besides the sheer numbers of Japanese left dead, the survivor accounts and photographs of the two cities were chilling. Perhaps the harshest reality, however, was that a bomb of such magnitude had been used on innocent civilians. An attack of this breadth on civilians was unprecedented, and it generated fear that anyone whose enemy possessed these weapons was in serious danger. Although the Americans were feared first, it was not long before other nations began building nuclear weapons so that they, too, would demand fearful respect.

Despite its position as a world leader with a strong military, America also lost its sense of security during the 1940s. This new sense of uncertainty provided the foundation for the heightened suspicion between the United States and the Soviet Union at the end of the war. When British prime minister Winston Churchill delivered his famous "Iron Curtain" speech in 1946, he articulated the political and ideological division between the Western world and the Soviet Union. Distrust flourished as the frightening realization set in that the Soviet Union could and would oppose the United States.

When the Soviet Union made great technological strides in strategic areas such as weapons development and space exploration, America's fear became more pronounced. The greater the advances made by the Soviet Union, the harder the United States worked to outpace the Soviets, and vice versa. During the Cold War, these two superpowers devoted vast resources to building bigger and better bombs. In a way, it was a high-stakes game to see who would blink first.

The Soviets were seen as a threat on virtually every front—political philosophy, weaponry, and then science. In 1957 the Soviets won an important leg of the space race by successfully launching the first satellite to orbit the earth. The satellite, *Sputnik*, was a symbolic victory for the Soviets and a black eye for Americans, who had always believed themselves to be the world's technological leaders. That the Soviets reached this goal first made many Americans ask themselves what other advances the Soviets had made. Were the Soviets close to asserting superiority over the United States, and if so, was America in danger? These were the worries that plagued the American psyche and continued to undercut American confidence.

President Harry S. Truman's "containment policy" gave voice to the American resolve to prevent the spread of communism in the world. This resolve turned into action in the Korean War (1950–1953), during which American troops went to support South Koreans who fought against advancing North Korean Communist troops.

The ideological conflict between democracy and communism was at the heart of the Cold War. Spreading their own ideologies became the basis for the U.S. and Soviet attempts to win the hearts and minds of other nations. In a sense, the two superpowers were vying for control of the world's support. Violent Cold War outbreaks were inevitable on the world stage, and they erupted in Cuba, Korea, and Vietnam. Long after 1960 came to a close, the Cold War was still driving international conflict.

Between 1940 and 1960, the world gained a new understanding of leadership in all its forms through a historic lineup of world leaders. Many of these leaders are still revered today, such as Winston Churchill (who ascended to the position of England's prime minister twice during this period) and Martin Luther King Jr. Leaders such as Harry S. Truman, General Douglas MacArthur, Mao Zedong, and Nikita Khrushchev continue to spark debate. And perhaps the most reviled world leader to date, Adolf Hitler, ascended to the height of his power during the events of the 1940s.

Besides the losses and gains, the overriding themes of the era have become hallmarks of today's societies and national identities. Europeans remain steadfast in their resolve to remember the Holocaust and never allow it to happen again. Throughout the 1950s, European nations worked to find a way to unite in their weakness in order to gain strength. In the wake of World War II, they needed each other for economic survival. In 1957 the European Economic Community (EEC) was formed as a way of running a cooperative market in Europe. This spirit of economic unity kept the EEC alive and well for many years, but nationalists had an even bigger dream for Europe. In 1993 the EEC became the European Union, which meant not only market-based cooperation but also more universalization in currency, law, professional accreditation, and policy making.

Americans came out of these years with greater wisdom and

determination not to repeat certain mistakes. When terrorists attacked the United States on September 11, 2001, for example, numerous commentators compared it to the attack on Pearl Harbor. Both were surprise attacks, and both took place on American soil. As Arab Americans endured racism and suspicion, many Americans were quick to caution against the kind of panic that enabled the Japanese internment and the McCarthy hearings. Still, the same insecurity and fear felt by Americans after Pearl Harbor was felt by Americans after the terrorist attacks. Arab Americans held in military prisons became the focus of impassioned debates about what it means to be an American. As of this writing, attorneys continue to try their cases in the legal arena.

Other episodes from 1940 to 1960 shape society today. The first war-crime trials, the Nuremberg trials, held Nazis accountable for their war crimes. Today, war crimes remain an important topic in international affairs, and combatants are expected to follow international law on such matters. In high schools all across the country, students learn about optimism in the face of devastation as they read Anne Frank's diary. The civil rights movement, which had its roots in the 1950s segregated South, is still alive and well in the efforts of special interest groups doggedly pursuing equality and justice for everyone. Although the space race is over, space programs all over the world continue to make progress in the area of space exploration.

Just as it is human nature to change and grow with each hard lesson learned, so it is with humankind in general. During the years between 1940 and 1960, not only did America change in very profound and permanent ways, but so did the world. The world was a markedly different place in 1961 than it had been in 1939, and those changes continue to shape attitudes and behavior today. Whether discussing popular culture, music, politics, civil rights, technology, or literature, important and relevant roots are located squarely in these two decades. Few eras contain as many intense events as these years; between the crucibles of World War II and the Cold War, millions of people's lives were altered in ways they never imagined. Having seen the most evil and the noblest of human endeavor, people at the time were fundamentally changed. Today, people from all walks of life are drawn to this era and its many intriguing facets. So powerful are the events that anyone who studies history inevitably becomes engrossed in the events of these two decades.

The Bombing of Pearl Harbor:
December 7, 1941

Pearl Harbor Changes the Course of World War II

by Susanne Everett, Peter Young, and Robin Sommer

In 1940 and 1941, increasingly militant and aggressive government leaders rose to power in Japan. Their support of Germany in the war in Europe created diplomatic tension with the United States, whose leaders denounced the Third Reich and its supporters.

To most Americans, the war in Europe was tragic but distant, and they had no reason to expect military attacks. After all, the United States had not declared war on anyone, nor had anyone declared war on the United States. On Saturday, December 6, 1941, a large portion of the naval fleet was docked in Pearl Harbor, located on the Hawaiian island of Oahu. In all, there were ninety-four ships, including eight battleships. The next morning, at 7:55, Japanese bombers began a surprise attack on Pearl Harbor. A single squadron of American fighter planes and a few small naval vessels managed to get in position to defend against the attackers, but the fleet was exposed and vulnerable. By the time the Japanese bombers departed at 9:45 A.M., 188 planes were destroyed, all eight battleships were either damaged or destroyed, and numerous smaller vessels were rendered useless. In contrast, the Japanese lost only five midget submarines, one full-size submarine, and twenty-nine of its almost two hundred planes. The human toll at Pearl Harbor was sobering; almost thirty-

Susanne Everett, Peter Young, and Robin Sommer, *Wars of the Twentieth Century: World War I, World War II, the Korean War, the Vietnam War, the Middle East War*. London: Bison Books, 1985. Copyright © 1985 by Bison Books, Ltd. Reproduced by permission of Susanne Everett Keegan.

four hundred Americans lost their lives, and more than eleven hundred were wounded. The events of that morning set into motion a series of events that would change the course of World War II.

From the Japanese perspective, the attack was a disappointment because it did not destroy any aircraft carriers and it left massive fuel oil storage facilities intact. From the American perspective, the attack meant that the United States would join in the war effort with the Allies. This was significant because the Americans had a large military, plenty of resources and equipment, and advanced technologies.

This selection is taken from *Wars of the Twentieth Century*, by Susanne Everett, Peter Young, and Robin Sommer. Everett is a British historian who is the author of *World War I: An Illustrated History.* Young was a British military leader during World War II, distinguishing himself in such operations as the Normandy invasion. Upon retirement from the military, Young accepted a position as head of the War Studies department at the Royal Military Academy. He is the author of more than twenty books on military endeavors. Sommer is an American writer who has edited and coauthored numerous books on historical subjects.

We, by the grace of heaven, Emperor of Japan, seated on the Throne of a line unbroken for ages eternal, enjoin upon ye, Our loyal and brave subjects:

We hereby declare war on the United States of America and the British Empire. The men and officers of Our Army and Navy shall do their utmost in prosecuting the war, Our public servants of various departments shall perform faithfully and diligently their appointed tasks, and all other subjects of Ours shall pursue their respective duties; the entire nation with a united will shall mobilize their total strength so that nothing will miscarry in the attainment of our war aims.

> Imperial Rescript: the 8th day of the
> 12th month of the 16th year of Shava

The Japanese did not await this pronouncement before beginning their war in a somewhat less formal way. Like their Nazi and Fascist allies they struck the first blow without warning. . . .

Pearl Harbor Succeeded and Failed

Only one thing marred for the Japanese their tactical success at Pearl Harbor; they neither damaged nor sank a single carrier, for the simple reason that they [the carriers] were out of an exercise. And it was the carrier, not the battleship, that was to be the vital warship of the Pacific War, for deprived of their battleships the Americans made a virtue of necessity and fought a new kind of war.

From the point of view of grand strategy Pearl Harbor was a disastrous blunder. The Americans could take hard knocks, but they did not care to be the victims of low cunning. They had not wanted war. However anxious [President Franklin D.] Roosevelt may have been to aid the victims of Nazi and Fascist aggression, they did not wish to become involved. The aftermath of isolation was still strong. But now at a blow the Japanese put the nation right behind their President, and that farseeing statesman lost no time in denouncing 7 December as 'a date which will live in infamy', and in declaring that the war was all one, whether against the Japanese or against [Nazi leader Adolf] Hitler and [Italian dictator Benito] Mussolini. Congress voted for war against Japan without a single speech or one dissentient voice.

Pearl Harbor Escalated the World War

Far away in Berlin the German Foreign Minister, [Joachim] von Ribbentrop, was jubilant. Mussolini too was happy. [Italian foreign affairs minister] Count [Galeazzo] Ciano, more intelligent than either, saw that America would now enter the European conflict, which would be so long that she would be able to bring all her potential forces to bear. On 11 December Germany and Italy declared war on the United States, which returned the compliment.

Latin America was thoroughly aroused by these events, and within the next few days Costa Rica, the Dominican Republic, Haiti, Honduras, Nicaragua, El Salvador, Cuba, Guatemala and Panama all declared war on the Axis.

The Scales Tipped in Favor of the Allies

It is no more than realistic to recognize that 7 December 1941 was one of the most significant days in British history: the day that put the United States squarely in the war as an ally. The war had now been going on for more than two years, years during which Britain had won few enough victories to set off against a multitude of German triumphs. It is true that the British had always been confident of ultimate victory; this conviction was certainly an asset but it was not altogether logical. And it is true that Hitler had dealt himself a deadly blow on the day he invaded Russia. But now by their attack on Pearl Harbor the Japanese ranged the most powerful of all possible allies on the British side. Whatever disasters lay in store—and there were plenty—the most pessimistic of Britons could no longer suppose that the Allies could lose.

But the way ahead was still a long one, and the United States, like Britain, was to pay a sorry price for years of pacifism and isolationism. . . .

The Japanese Seized the Momentum of Success

The Japanese were swift to exploit their success at Pearl Harbor. In the Central Pacific they overwhelmed the small US garrison of Guam (10 December) and on 23 December, after one bloody repulse (11 December) and a long and heavy bombardment, invaded Wake Island, where some 500 United States Marines under Major James Devereux put up a magnificent resistance.

Next the Japanese struck at the Philippines, where General Douglas MacArthur was in command. MacArthur, who had been Chief of the US Army Staff, had no illusions as to the likelihood of war with Japan, and had done all that lay in his power to prepare his command. He had at his disposal about 200 aircraft, including 35 Flying Fortresses, 19,000 American troops and 11,000 Philippine Scouts. The newly-raised Philippine Army, which was as yet of little military value, numbered about 160,000.

The 7,083 islands of the Philippine Archipelago had been annexed by the United States after Admiral [George] Dewey's victory over the Spanish Fleet in Manila Bay during the Spanish-American War (1898). The biggest islands are Luzon and Mindanao. The Americans had promised to give independence to this considerable part of their empire by 1946.

Japan Strikes the Philippines

The preliminary air bombardment destroyed many of the American planes. On 10 December the Japanese began to land on the north coast of Luzon, following up with yet another landing on the east coast.

Clouds of smoke engulf the battleship *West Virginia*
following the Japanese attack on Pearl Harbor.

On 27 December General MacArthur reported to Washington:

'Enemy penetration in the Philippines resulted from out of weakness in the sea and in the air. Surface elements of the Asiatic Fleet
were withdrawn and the effect of submarines has been negligible.
Lack of airfields for modern planes prevented defensive dispersion
and lack of pursuit planes permitted unhindered day bombardment.
The enemy has had utter freedom of naval and air movements.'

On the same day Manila was declared an open city. This did
not save it from a destructive air bombardment which lasted two
days. On 2 January the Japanese occupied the city and the naval
base of Cavite.

In January MacArthur now withdrew some 40,000 men into
the Bataan Peninsula where he had always intended to make his
last stand. Bataan, which is about 25 miles long by 20 miles

wide, juts out from Luzon. The Americans attempted to supply
MacArthur by blockade-runners, but none got through. In February he was ordered to Australia, and much against his will
went to take over the South-West Pacific Area. The Japanese
broke through the Bataan position on 31 March and 9 April
35,000 Americans laid down their arms. The prisoners were
treated with bestial cruelty in the notorious death march that followed. Lieutenant-General Jonathan Wainwright held out in the
old Spanish island fortress of Corregidor until 6 May, denying
the enemy the use of Manila Bay, one of the best natural har-
bours in the East.

By their conquest of the Philippines the Japanese had destroyed an army of at least 90,000 men. . . .

Japanese Confidence

The first six months of their war had gone so well for the Japanese that they were seriously misled as to its future course. The
victories of their Nazi allies and their contempt for democracy
alike led them to undervalue their enemies. Russia seemed unlikely to survive; Britain, on the defensive against Germany,
could do Japan no harm; America, crippled by Pearl Harbor and
politically decadent, would eventually come to terms.

Americans Fight Back Against Japan

But grave though the situation was, the Americans were already
striking back. Admiral Chester W. Nimitz, who had succeeded
Admiral [Husband] Kimmel on 31 December 1941, had lost no
time in restoring the morale of his command. . . .

Nimitz saw that for the time being hit-and-run raids, similar
to those that the British were making on the coasts of Europe,
were the only form of offensive action he could take. In the Pacific the aircraft carrier took the place of the commando. On 1
February 1942 Admiral [William] Halsey's group, built up round
the carrier *Enterprise,* attacked Kwajalein in the Marshall Islands, and besides killing the Japanese commander sank a transport and damaged nine other vessels.

Admiral Wilson Brown's *Lexington* group raided Rabaul and
brought on an air battle in which the Americans won the upper
hand (20 February). On 10 March this force, with the *Yorktown*
added, raided Lae and Salamaua on the North coast of Papua.

But the raid that really puzzled the Japanese came on 18 April, when Lieutenant-Colonel James H. Doolittle and 16 B-25 Mitchells flew 668 miles from the carrier *Hornet,* bombed Tokyo, and flew on to land in China. The actual damage inflicted was not very great, but the effect on American morale was tonic. Moreover the Japanese now allotted hundreds of planes to the defence of Tokyo, for they could not guess where the planes had flown from.

Roosevelt Declares War on Japan

by Franklin D. Roosevelt

Franklin D. Roosevelt was president for twelve years (1933– 1945), the longest administration in American history. During his years in the Oval Office, he guided a distraught nation through the Great Depression with his New Deal programs, which helped to create jobs and provide much-needed relief for the unemployed. Once domestic affairs were in order, however, Roosevelt's attention turned sharply toward Europe and Adolf Hitler, whose land grabs and 1940 attacks on France and Britain revealed him as a well-armed aggressor. Despite Congress's reluctance to get involved in the expanding world war, Roosevelt supported European resistance to the Third Reich by sending war matériel, destroyers, and money to Britain.

Congress became convinced of the need for U.S. involvement on December 7, 1941, after the Japanese launched a surprise attack at Pearl Harbor. This unexpected and unprecedented attack on American soil struck terror in the hearts of all Americans, and it was up to Roosevelt to take quick and decisive action. The next day, he stood before Congress and requested that its members declare war on Japan. This speech demonstrates Roosevelt's passion and rage. He had no tolerance for the hypocrisy of the stealth attack, and he was committed to protecting America from future attacks. His phrase "a date which will live in infamy" has become historic and, to many Americans, almost inseparable from the event itself.

Roosevelt proved a reassuring presence to the American people, and his support of the war effort was thorough. Not only did he ensure the military had the resources it needed to wage war in foreign lands, but he also kept domestic efforts focused to support the soldiers overseas. Factories were kept running to produce supplies nec-

---

Franklin D. Roosevelt, "War Message to Congress, Washington, D.C., December 8, 1941," *Nothing to Fear: The Selected Addresses of Franklin Delano Roosevelt, 1932–1945*, edited by B.D. Zevin. Boston: Houghton Mifflin Company, 1946.

essary for the war effort, and citizens were implored to do their parts in small and big ways. The result was an enormous sense of unity. Roosevelt suffered a massive and fatal cerebral hemorrhage on April 12, 1945. His work toward Allied victory and establishing the United Nations would be fulfilled after his death.

Yesterday, December 7, 1941—a date which will live in infamy—the United States of America was suddenly and deliberately attacked by naval and air forces of the Empire of Japan.

The United States was at peace with that nation and, at the solicitation of Japan, was still in conversation with its government and its Emperor looking toward the maintenance of peace in the Pacific. Indeed, one hour after Japanese air squadrons had commenced bombing in Oahu, the Japanese ambassador to the United States and his colleague delivered to the Secretary of State a formal reply to a recent American message. While this reply stated that it seemed useless to continue the existing diplomatic negotiations, it contained no threat or hint of war or armed attack.

It will be recorded that the distance of Hawaii from Japan makes it obvious that the attack was deliberately planned many days or even weeks ago. During the intervening time the Japanese Government has deliberately sought to deceive the United States by false statements and expressions of hope for continued peace.

The attack yesterday on the Hawaiian Islands has caused severe damage to American naval and military forces. Very many American lives have been lost. In addition American ships have been reported torpedoed on the high seas between San Francisco and Honolulu.

Yesterday the Japanese government also launched an attack against Malaya.

Last night Japanese forces attacked Hong Kong.

Last night Japanese forces attacked Guam.

Last night Japanese forces attacked the Philippine Islands.

Last night the Japanese attacked Wake Island.

This morning the Japanese attacked Midway Island.

Japan has, therefore, undertaken a surprise offensive extending throughout the Pacific area. The facts of yesterday speak for themselves. The people of the United States have already formed their opinions and well understand the implications to the very life and safety of our nation.

Requesting a Declaration of War

As Commander-in-Chief of the Army and Navy, I have directed that all measures be taken for our defense.

Always will we remember the character of the onslaught against us.

No matter how long it may take us to overcome this premeditated invasion, the American people in their righteous might will win through to absolute victory.

I believe I interpret the will of the Congress and of the people when I assert that we will not only defend ourselves to the utmost but will make very certain that this form of treachery shall never endanger us again.

Hostilities exist. There is no blinking at the fact that our people, our territory and our interests are in grave danger.

With confidence in our armed forces—with the unbounding determination of our people—we will gain the inevitable triumph—so help us God.

I ask that the Congress declare that since the unprovoked and dastardly attack by Japan on Sunday, December 7th, a state of war has existed between the United States and the Japanese Empire.

Japanese Americans Are Sent to Internment Camps: February 19, 1942

Ordering the Internment of Japanese Americans

by Franklin D. Roosevelt

Two months after the surprise attack on Pearl Harbor by the Japanese and the subsequent declaration of war against Japan, President Franklin D. Roosevelt issued Executive Order 9066. This order gave the military the authority to remove people who posed potential security risks from designated zones and provide shelter and accommodations for displaced people. The latitude given to the military in this document was wide and allowed for Japanese Americans in areas along the Pacific Coast to be placed in internment camps built in the rural West.

Ten camps were constructed, and approximately 112,000 Japanese Americans of all ages went to live in them. These camps were located in California, Arizona, Colorado, Utah, Wyoming, and Arkansas. Upon receiving orders to report for registration, people had between two days and two weeks to send word to family and friends and sell or find a place to store all their belongings. Often, this meant selling valuables for a fraction of their worth and abandoning homes and property.

Japanese internment has become a shameful chapter in American history. Of the 112,000 detainees, 70,000 were American citizens. In fact, many of the young people were actually born in the United States. They considered themselves American, not Japanese, and

---

Franklin D. Roosevelt, Executive Order 9066, February 19, 1942.

many of their families had worked very hard to come to America so their children could be Americans. Besides ordering thousands of people to live in the camps, the government was among those who took advantage of their powerlessness and desperation. When detainees were finally released upon the end of the war in 1945, they were given only twenty-five dollars and train fare. Some estimates of the value of property, belongings, and income lost by Japanese Americans during the internment total billions of dollars. In 1988 President Ronald Reagan extended a formal apology on behalf of the government to the Japanese American detainees. He also offered twenty thousand dollars to each surviving victim as compensation.

The last camp, Tule Lake, closed in 1946, seven months after the end of the war.

W hereas the successful prosecution of the war requires every possible protection against espionage and against sabotage to national-defense material, national-defense premises, and national-defense utilities as defined in Section 4, Act of April 20, 1918, 40 Stat. 533, as amended by the Act of November 30, 1940, 54 Stat. 1220, and the Act of August 21, 1941, 55 Stat. 655 (U.S.C., Title 50, Sec 104):

Now, therefore, by virtue of the authority vested in me as President of the United States, and Commander in Chief of the Army and Navy, I hereby authorize and direct the Secretary of War, and the Military Commanders whom he may from time to time designate, whenever he or any designated Commander deems such action necessary or desirable, to prescribe military areas in such places and of such extent as he or the appropriate Military Commander may determine, from which any or all persons may be excluded, and with respect to which, the right of any person to enter, remain in, or leave shall be subject to whatever restrictions the Secretary of War or the appropriate Military Commander may determine, from which any or all persons may be excluded, and with respect to which, the right of any person to enter, remain in, or leave shall be subject to whatever restrictions the Secretary of War or the appropriate Military Commander may impose in his discretion. The Secretary of War is hereby authorized to provide for residents of any such area who are excluded therefrom, such transportation, food, shelter, and other accommoda-

During the internment of Japanese Americans, many families were forced to abandon their businesses and sell their belongings for a fraction of their worth.

tions as may be necessary, in the judgment of the Secretary of War or the said Military Commander, and until other arrangements are made, to accomplish the purpose of this order. The designation of military areas in any region or locality shall supersede designations of prohibited and restricted areas by the Attorney General under the Proclamations of December 7 and 8, 1941, and shall supersede the responsibility and authority of the Attorney General under the said Proclamations in respect of such prohibited and restricted areas.

I hereby further authorize and direct the Secretary of War and said Military Commanders to take such other steps as he or the appropriate Military Commander may deem advisable to enforce compliance with the restrictions applicable to each military area hereinabove authorized to be designated, including the use of

Federal troops and other Federal Agencies, with authority to accept assistance of state and local agencies.

I hereby further authorize and direct all Executive Departments, independent establishments and other Federal Agencies, to assist the Secretary of War or the said Military Commanders in carrying out this Executive Order, including the furnishing of medical aid, hospitalization, food, clothing, transportation, use of land, shelter, and other supplies, equipment, utilities, facilities, and services.

This order shall not be construed as modifying or limiting in any way the authority heretofore granted under Executive Order No. 8972, dated December 12, 1941, nor shall it be construed as limiting or modifying the duty and responsibility of the Federal Bureau of Investigation, with respect to the investigation of alleged acts of sabotage or the duty and responsibility of the Attorney General and the Department of Justice under the Proclamations of December 7 and 8, 1941, prescribing regulations for the conduct and control of alien enemies, except as such duty and responsibility is superseded by the designation of military areas hereunder.

Former Japanese American Detainees Recall the Camps

by Emmy E. Werner

In February 1942 Japanese Americans of all ages were forced to abandon their homes to go live in internment camps. There were ten camps in all, and more than one hundred thousand people lived in them between 1942 and 1946. Living conditions were cramped and harsh, and detainees often had to compete for resources and facilities. Because the camps were built in western desert areas, the temperatures swung wildly from below zero at night to well over one hundred degrees during the day. Families shared tiny apartments, and childless couples who did not know each other often had to live together. Shower and toilet facilities were rustic, and meals were served in communal dining rooms. Outside the camps, the view was also bleak. Barbed wire and armed guards reminded detainees that they were, in effect, prisoners of war.

Emmy E. Werner was a little girl in Germany during World War II. Her personal memories of the war are strong, but she is also interested in the experience of other children during the war. For her book *Through the Eyes of Innocents: Children Witness World War II*, from which this selection is excerpted, she collected the writings of children during the war (diaries, poems, and letters) to complement her interviews with adults recalling their wartime experiences. The following excerpts are those she assembled to tell the stories of children sent to Japanese internment camps. Some are writings from the war years and others are excerpts from interviews with

Emmy E. Werner, *Through the Eyes of Innocents: Children Witness World War II*. Boulder, CO: Westview Press, 2000. Copyright © 2000 by Westview Press, a Member of the Perseus Books Group. Reproduced by permission.

adult Japanese Americans who spent childhood years in the camps. These excerpts reveal how the camps affected their social lives, emotions, cultural identities, and family dynamics.

Most of the Japanese Americans removed from their homes for reasons of "national security" were school-age children, infants, and teenagers too young to vote. Two-thirds had been born in the United States. None had committed crimes against their government—yet they were collectively ordered to report for internment and faced the staggering necessity of leaving all they had known, owned, and loved.

The Fujimoto Family

My colleague, Isao Fujimoto, is one of the gentlest persons I have ever known. Born on the Yakima Indian Reservation in the state of Washington, he was in the third grade when the United States entered World War II. He remembers:

> Right after Pearl Harbor, the FBI came to our home, and my father just disappeared. I remember the last words he was saying was, "Oh, let me put my pants on." That was it. He was put in the Yakima County Jail. Then he was sent to a Detention Center in Missoula, Montana. . . . I didn't see him until about a year-and-a-half later. My mother asked me to write a letter to President [Franklin D.] Roosevelt. I wrote him about our situation. All of us were still farming, and though my father disappeared in December, come Spring we put in the crops. The question is what do we do next? So I wrote to Roosevelt saying that it would be very good if my father came back because we really needed help here. My mother was only twenty-five years old at the time, and there were five kids. We were farming using horses. It was very hard if you're small, and you can't really hook up a plow. So I told the President that it would help a lot if my father could return to his family. Of course, I never got a reply. . . . I was eight years old at the time.

The Fujimoto family would not be planting or harvesting any more crops for the duration of the war. On March 2, 1942, the commander of the Western Defense Command, empowered by President Roosevelt's Executive Order 9066, designated Washington, Oregon, California, and parts of Arizona "strategic military areas." He ordered all persons of Japanese descent who lived there removed from their homes. They were allowed to take with them only what they could carry.

The Mass Evacuation

On March 31, 1942, the evacuation began, first to assembly centers, where the average stay lasted about 100 days, then to hastily constructed relocation centers. Thirteen of the sixteen assembly centers were in California; the other three were in Washington, Oregon, and Arizona.

For many Japanese American children who were evacuated from the West Coast, the most traumatic experience was leaving behind their beloved pets, since animals were not allowed to go with them. One boy wrote about leaving his collie: "He knew something was wrong. . . . He suspected because we were carrying our suitcases with us. When we were going down our garden . . . he followed us. I told him to go home. He just sat and howled and cried. My cousin and I got mad at him but we love him almost as much as if he were a human being. . . . When we drove away from the front of the house he was sitting inside the fence looking out."

Grace Nakamura, testifying in 1981 to the Commission on Wartime Relocation and Internment of Civilians, recalled her trip:

On May 16, 1942, at 9:30 A.M. we departed . . . for an unknown destination. To this day I can remember vividly the plight of the elderly, some on stretchers, orphans herded on the train by caretakers, and especially a young couple with four preschool children. The mother had two frightened toddlers hanging on to her coat. In her arms, she carried two crying babies. The father had diapers and other baby paraphernalia strapped to his back. In his hands he struggled with dufflebag and suitcase. The shades were drawn on the train for our entire trip. Military police patrolled the aisles.

To this day, child evacuees often recall two images of their arrival at the assembly centers: a cordon of armed guards and the barbed wire and searchlights, symbols of a prison. Many families arrived at the assembly centers incomplete. In some cases, as was true for Isao Fujimoto, fathers had earlier been taken into custody by the FBI. Peter Ota, sixteen, and his thirteen-year-old sister traveled by themselves. Their father had been detained and their mother was in a tuberculosis sanitorium, where they were allowed to visit her only once in four and a half months.

Making the Best of a Harsh Situation

One of the most severe discomforts of the assembly centers was the lack of privacy. Eight-person families were placed in 20-by-20-foot rooms; six persons, like Isao's family, in 12-by-20-foot rooms; and four persons in 8-by-20-foot rooms. Within the confines of the assembly centers, the Japanese American evacuees tried to create a community. They organized schools, sport programs, talent shows. Yet even the youngest knew they were no longer free.

A young girl wrote about her life in the shadows of the guard towers at the Tanforan Assembly Center in California:

> We have roll call about 6:30 every day. I'm at the rec hall every day before roll call we are playing basketball or swinging on the bars. When the siren rings I get so scared that I sometimes scream, some people gets scared of me instead of the siren. We run home as fast as I could then we wait about 5 minutes, when the inspectors come to check that we are all home. . . . After the camp roll call finish the siren rings again. . . . I hate roll call because it scares you too much.

Ironically, Independence Day was cause for elaborate celebrations among the children. Sachi Kajiwara described her preparation for the Fourth of July at Tanforan:

> I worked as a recreation leader in our block of 7–10 year-old girls. Perhaps one of the highlights was the yards and yards of paper chains we (my 7–10 year-old girls) made from cut-up strips of newspapers which we colored red, white and blue for the big Fourth of July dance. . . . These paper chains were the decoration that festooned the walls of the Recreation Hall. It was our Independence Day celebration, though we were behind barbed wire, military police all around us, and we could see the big sign of *South San Francisco* on the hill just outside of the Tanforan Assembly Center.

The Relocation Camps

In the late summer and fall of 1942, the assembly centers were emptied and their tenants were loaded onto trains and sent to relocation centers in Manzanar and Tule Lake, California; Poston and Gila, Arizona; Topaz, Utah; Minidoka, Idaho; Heart Mountain, Wyoming; Granada, Colorado; and Jerome and Rohwer, Arkansas. Like the assembly centers, the relocation centers were inadequate in size, sanitation, and protection from the elements.

They were located in the most God-forsaken regions of the United States, exposing the evacuees to windblown deserts, blistering summers, and freezing winters. At Poston, Arizona, summer temperatures reached 115 degrees; at Minidoka, Idaho, they averaged 110 degrees. In the relocation centers in Wyoming and Colorado, winter temperatures fell to minus 30 degrees. The centers in Arkansas were in damp, swampy lowlands where poisonous snakes made their home.

A young girl, Itsuko Taniguchi, described in a poem her journey to "the land with lots of sand":

My Mom, Pop, & me
Us living three
Dreaded the day
When we rode away,
Away to the land
With lots of sand
My mom, pop, & me
The day of evacuation
We left our little station
Leaving our friends
And my tree that bends
Away to the land
With lots of sand
My mom, pop, & me.

In August 1942, Isao Fujimoto's mother and her five children, ranging in age from eight years to ten months, made the trip from the Portland Assembly Center to the Heart Mountain Relocation Center on a rickety train accompanied by armed guards. Isao recalls:

Once we got to Heart Mountain, I remember how traumatic it was because we got separated again. My youngest sister Keiko had measles, so she was quarantined. My mother had to be with her. When we got taken to the barracks, I didn't know where my mother was. I wandered all over the camp looking for her. I found her. I don't know how. . . . I discovered her in an empty barrack sitting all by herself with my [baby] sister.

Orphans and Foster Children

Keiko was not the only infant who would spend years of her life in a concentration camp. One hundred and one Japanese Ameri-

can orphans and foster children—some as young as six months—
were quietly rounded up by the U.S. Army during the summer of
1942. These children, some with only one-eighth Japanese ancestry, were sent to a hastily built children's village at the Manzanar Relocation Center in southern California. A number of them
had been in the care of Catholic nuns in the Maryknoll Home for
Japanese Children in Los Angeles. Father Hugh T. Lavery of the
Catholic Maryknoll Center was so taken back by the harshness of
the commandant presiding over the uprooting of the orphans that
he wrote a letter to President [Harry] Truman after the war, pro-
testing the man's confirmation as undersecretary of the army:
"Colonel Bendetsen showed himself to be a little Hitler. I mentioned that we had an orphanage with children of Japanese ancestry, and that some of these children were half Japanese, others
one fourth or less. I asked which children should we send. . . .
Bendetsen said 'I am determined that if they have *one* drop of
Japanese blood in them, they must go to camp.'". . .

On Thanksgiving Day 1942, the director of the Manzanar Relocation Center, Ralph P. Merritt, visited the orphans and was
greatly moved by the youngsters' fate. He wrote in his daily
notes: "The morning was spent at the Children's Village with the
90 orphans [to date] who had been evacuated from Alaska to San
Diego and sent to Manzanar because they might be a threat to
national security. What a travesty of justice!"

Manzanar

Located some 210 miles northeast of Los Angeles in the California desert, surrounded by sand, sage, and Joshua trees, Manzanar was the first of the relocation centers to which Japanese
American evacuees were sent. It was also the largest center—
holding, at its peak, over ten thousand men, women, and children. Surrounded by barbed wire, it was guarded by eight towers with machine guns. No area within the center was beyond the
reach of a soldier's bullet, not even at night, when searchlights
continually scanned the brush.

The center covered one square mile and was divided into
thirty-six blocks, with twenty-four barracks to each block. Each
barrack was 20 feet wide and 120 feet long. Laundry and bathroom facilities were located in the center of each block, each of
which had an open mess hall. Soldiers marched the new arrivals
to the mess hall, where their numbers were recorded. Guards

searched them, seizing anything they considered dangerous—
kitchen knives, knitting needles, even hot plates for warming babies' milk.

Each internee was issued a cot, an army blanket, and a sack to
be filled with straw for a mattress; then families were assigned to
a barrack according to size and number of children. A family of
four lived in a 20-by-25-foot space; two couples without children
shared one space, with only sheets hung as partitions to separate
them. Soon, lids from tin cans became items highly valued by all
Japanese American families in the center. They nailed them over
knotholes in the floor and walls to repel the desert winds. No one
ever completely overcame the relentless onslaught of desert grit.

The 250 people living in a block shared common bathroom facilities. On a concrete slab, down the center room, toilet bowls
were arranged in pairs, back-to-back, with no partitions. Teenagers, especially, resented this loss of privacy and identity. Only
after many complaints were the toilets partitioned. . . .

Getting to the mess hall on time; finding an empty shower;
keeping the baby's diapers clean; and coping with the heat, dust,
and insects were major tasks. Holding the family together without privacy required a full-time commitment. So did the evacuees' determination to get an education for their children. . . .

As the months turned into years, the center began to resemble
an American small town, with schools, churches, fire and police
departments, Boy Scouts, baseball leagues, and glee clubs. Outside the regular school sessions and the recreation programs sponsored by the WRA [War Relocation Authority], classes of every
kind were being offered: singing, acting, trumpet playing, tap-
dancing. Observed Jeanne Wakatsuki: "The fact that America had
accused us, or excluded us, or imprisoned us, or whatever it might
be called, did not change the kind of world we wanted. Most of
us were born in this country; we had no other models.". . .

John Tateishi, in his *Remembrances of Manzanar*, sums up the
paradoxical experience of growing up as an American-born child
of Japanese descent within the confines of a detention camp:

> In some ways, I suppose, my life was not too different from a lot
> of kids in America between the years 1942 and 1945. I spent a
> good part of my time playing with my brothers and friends,
> learned to shoot marbles, watched sandlot baseball and envied the
> older kids who wore Boy Scout uniforms. . . . We imported much

of America into the camps, because, after all, we *were* Americans. Through imitation of my brothers, who attended grade school in the camp, I learned to salute the flag by the time I was five years old. I was learning, as best one could learn in Manzanar, what it meant to live in America. But, I was also learning the sometimes bitter price one has to pay for it.

Topaz

. . . The Japanese American children from the San Francisco Bay Area were sent to Topaz, a three-day trip by train from San Bruno, California, to a harsh windblown desert near the town of Delta in Utah. . . .

Yoshiko Uchida, a young student from the University of California at Berkeley, worked as prison camp teacher, both at the Tanforan Assembly Center and the Topaz Relocation Center. In her book *The Invisible Thread*, Uchida chronicled her experiences teaching Japanese American children in barracks cold as a refrigerator with wailing winds that poured buckets full of sand through holes of the roof of her classroom. She also remembered happier times, especially her "Concentration Camp Christmas," when there were decorated trees, special food, and presents donated by the Quakers.

> The day before Christmas a large carton of greens arrived for my mother from her friends in Connecticut. Opening it was like opening a door to an evergreen forest. It smelled glorious. It was the smell of Christmas. . . . That night, as I lay on my cot, surrounded by the fragrance of the fir sprays, listening to Christmas carols on the radio, I thought about how we would spend Christmas Day in a concentration camp. We would go to church, we would visit friends, and we would have a special turkey dinner at the mess hall without having to stand in line. As they had on Thanksgiving, the mess hall crew would serve us at our tables as a special treat.

Tule Lake

. . . For Isao Fujimoto and his family, 1944 would bring another move—this time from Heart Mountain, Wyoming, to Tule Lake in northern California, near the Oregon border. Isao's fate had been determined by his parents' answers to a WRA loyalty questionnaire. If the evacuees answered "Yes" to the questions "Will you stop pledging allegiance to Japan?" and "Would you serve

in the Armed Forces of the United States?" they were considered
loyal; if they answered "No," they were considered "disloyal."
The questions were posed to anybody over eighteen. Isao, then
ten years old, remembered:

> My mother and father did not want our family separated again. My
> father had been confined in [the Justice Department internment
> camp in] Missoula, Montana, and joined us at Heart Mountain
> about a year-and-a-half afterwards. So when the questionnaire was
> administered my parents decided [to answer] "No," "No." As a re-
> sult we were among the segregated families and sent to Tule Lake.
> . . . It was a very different kind of camp, because now you were
> not among people you knew. You were among people who had
> voted similarly on the loyalty test. The atmosphere was quite
> charged. . . . There were many kinds of organizations that were
> very pro-Japan. In fact, that became not only a dominating but a
> divisive force within Tule Lake. It set up an atmosphere of tension
> and intimidation.

Tule Lake was being transformed from a resettlement to a segregation center. A double eight-foot fence was erected; the guard
was increased to a battalion; and six tanks were lined up con-
spicuously. Within the camp, potential troublemakers were isolated in a detention center that was known as "the stockade.". . .
   At Tule Lake, Isao Fujimoto found himself in a relocation center that was not oriented toward the American mainstream, as had
been the case at Heart Mountain. Now he was placed in a setting
where there was much more emphasis on the Japanese culture
and martial arts. "The pro-Japanese people were very well organized," he remembered. "They even organized young kids but
my family was not into that." Instead the eleven-year-old boy
learned to live with contradictions in his daily life. In the morning he would go to the Japanese school, where he and his class-
mates assembled outside and started the day off by bowing to the
east—toward Japan. In the afternoon, he would attend the American school, where he and the other children would pledge allegiance to the American flag.
   "We thought nothing of it," he recalls. "For kids growing up,
you just go along. There were more important things [for me],
like baseball, collecting and trading stamps, and hunting for Indian arrowheads." When he came home from school or play, he
found the grown-ups in his block listening attentively to the

Japanese war news over a shortwave radio. "The propaganda came from the Japanese Ministry of War which was broadcasting all the victories. People took this all very seriously. They thought the war was going well."

Isao gained a different perspective from the teaching staff of the American school, who were his only contact with the outside world. And he discovered that his Japanese American compatriots were not the only ones who were behind barbed wire. On his way home from school one day he saw a group of Caucasians working alongside a ditch. "The strange part of it was that they were being bossed around [by MPs (military police)]. I asked, 'Who are these people?' They turned out to be prisoners of war (POWs). I learned later on that they were Italians captured in North Africa."

Many Japanese Americans Fought in the War

Even as the interns lived behind barbed wire, young Japanese American men served their country on battlefields in the Pacific and in Europe, and as interpreters, providing probably the most important link in American Intelligence. The 442nd Combat Team, an all Japanese American unit fighting in Italy and France, emerged with more casualties and more decorations for bravery than any other unit of comparable size and length of service in the army's history. One member of this unit was the teenager John Kanda, who had finished high school in Tule Lake.

The Detainees Are Finally Freed

On December 17, 1944, more than three years after the attack on Pearl Harbor, Japanese Americans finally regained their freedom to come and go to any part of the United States. The *San Francisco Chronicle* of Monday, December 19, 1944, announced the end of exclusion with these words: "The Western Defense Command yesterday lifted restrictions prohibiting the return of approximately 100,000 persons of Japanese ancestry excluded from California, Washington and Oregon in 1942 for reasons of military necessity. Exclusion has now been placed on a basis of individual loyalty instead of race."

The Normandy Invasion Was a Turning Point in the War

by Alan J. Levine

On June 6, 1944, the Allied forces launched a surprise amphibious landing on the beaches of Normandy in France. The attack on Normandy—known as D day—was unprecedented and required the efforts of top military, technological, and tactical minds. The assault was total, involving land, sea, and air troops and weapons. U.S. general Dwight D. Eisenhower, a war hero and future president (1952–1960), commanded the troops. Described by British prime minister Winston Churchill as the "most difficult and complicated operation ever to take place," the Normandy invasion was a crucial turning point in the war. It effectively sealed the fate of the German military and set the course of war toward an Allied victory.

On the morning of the invasion, an armada of more than five thousand ships delivered almost one hundred thousand troops to Normandy. Almost eleven hundred bombers and more than two thousand fighter planes also moved in. Factors such as the steep cliffs, strong German defense, and lack of air assault made it exceedingly difficult for American troops to make progress inland, but they made it. Their success, however, came at a high price; at Utah Beach there were two hundred casualties, and at Omaha Beach there were twenty-five hundred.

Alan J. Levine, *From the Normandy Beaches to the Baltic Sea: The Northwest Europe Campaign, 1944–1945*. Westport, CT: Praeger Publishers, 2000. Copyright © 2000 by Alan J. Levine. Reproduced by permission.

Because Adolf Hitler and Field Marshal Erwin Rommel suspected the Normandy invasion was a feint, intended to distract them from a more complete attack on Calais, they were unprepared for the attack. Once the Allies penetrated defenses at Normandy a few days later, they headed for Paris. After a hard-earned victory at Caen, Allied troops made it to Paris, liberating France on August 25. Within a year, the Allies had defeated Hitler's Germany.

Alan J. Levine is an author and historian with a special interest in World War II, Russian history, and international affairs. In addition to numerous articles about World War II and the Cold War, Levine is the author of *The Soviet Union, the Communist Movement, and the World: Prelude to the Cold War* (1992), *The Missile and Space Race* (1994), and *The War Against Rommel's Supply Lines, 1942–1943* (1999).

Since 1941 the leaders of the Western democracies had accepted that a land invasion of Western Europe was the only sure way to defeat Nazi Germany. The Allied leaders invested great resources in the strategic bombing of Germany, but whatever the leaders of the air forces believed and others hoped, Roosevelt, Churchill, and their principal advisers never counted on it to defeat Germany without an invasion on the ground. The air offensive was a way to prepare for and support a land attack, not an end in itself. Nor could the Western democracies, for many reasons, leave the land battle to the Red Army alone.

An attack through Western Europe afforded the shortest possible route to the heart of Germany, across relatively open terrain in an area with the best communications of any place in the world. . . .

The Allies had to land fairly close to Britain so that heavy fighter cover could be maintained, and they wanted to quickly take a port. They needed ample beaches, with some shelter against the weather, and easy exits that were not dominated by high ground. A major raid by the Canadians on Dieppe in 1942 had proven, at high cost, that the Allies dared not count on seizing a port directly from the sea. When the invasion was planned in 1943, the range of the then available fighters restricted an attack to the 300-mile front between the Scheldt and Cherbourg; planners knew that at least half the fighter cover would be supplied by short-range RAF [British Royal Air Force] Spitfires. The Dutch coast was beyond range, and unsuitable in other ways; Belgian beaches were few, small, and very heavily defended. The Calais area, closest to Britain, offered the best location for air cover, the shortest crossing of the Channel, and the shortest route to Germany. A landing there would drive a wedge between most of the German forces in the west and those nearer home. For these reasons, the Germans had planned to use it as the departure point for their planned invasion of England in 1940 and now viewed it as the likeliest target. It was therefore the most heavily defended area of the coast. It is still widely believed that Calais was the best point for an invasion and that the Allies rejected it only because it was too strongly held. But, quite aside from those defenses, the Allies found that Calais was far less attractive than it seemed at first sight. The short crossing was actually an illusion. The great harbors in Western Europe are either on the North Sea, well above the Straits of Dover, or well south of the Pas de Calais, on the western stretch of the Channel. A major Allied landing force would have to sail from ports far from the narrows and seize ports far from Calais. The Calais beaches, exposed and often poor, with narrow exits, were dominated by high ground. Expansion inland would be hard, and taking a major port—Le Havre or Antwerp—would involve an awkward move across the enemy front.

That left Normandy, with two major ports, Le Havre and Cherbourg. An attack on Le Havre would have to go ashore astride the Seine on inadequate beaches. The area near Cherbourg was too difficult to assault, but the Caen or Calvados coast had ample, sheltered beaches. Access to the interior was adequate, and there were good airfield sites near the shore. A force landing there could hope to take Cherbourg fairly soon. Although not perfect, Normandy was the best choice. The Allies worked very hard to hide this from the Germans. . . .

Allied Troops Arrive at Normandy

Finally the Allies were ready. June 5, 6, and 7 [1944] had the right combination of moonlight and tides, but the weather was bad. On June 5, Eisenhower had to decide whether to attack the next day, in marginal weather, or wait two more weeks. But there was no certainty that the weather would be better next time, and two weeks of campaigning time would have been lost. And the chances of the Germans learning the Normandy secret would grow. He gave the go-ahead. That was fortunate, for a storm erupted during the next "suitable" period. The machine was set into motion; the Allied commanders took their hands off the levers. Everything now depended on the navy and on the men going up the beaches and dropping out of the sky.

The bad weather exacted many penalties from the Allies, but it had one great dividend. It helped them achieve surprise. The Germans, already largely blinded by the Allied control of the air and sea and the bombing and jamming of their radar stations, were sure the Allies would not attack in such miserable conditions, particularly since they had just passed up such fine weather in May. Rommel and others were away from their commands, and the German Navy did not bother to send out "obviously" needless patrols.

Even the airborne landings, in the early hours of June 6, did not spark a full-scale reaction. The 4,500 ships and landing craft, carrying 160,000 men and supported by 11,000 planes, would arrive at their destination with far less warning than could reasonably have been expected.

Paratroopers Encounter Problems

The U.S. airborne divisions, with 16,000 men in the first drop, did not have an easy time, but did their jobs. Low clouds, turbulence, enemy flak, and badly trained troop-carrier crews combined to cause a very scattered drop. Yet the men collected themselves and began to carry out their assigned tasks, often with smaller forces than expected and with little coordination and firepower. That sometimes made things costly. A German squad, defending the strongly built stone buildings of a manor at La Fiere, stood off successive attacks by forces amounting to a full battalion simply because the various attackers, coming from different points of the compass, did not know of each other's existence, and had no heavy weapons. But the Americans finally secured the waterlines and bridgeheads needed to get out of Utah beach. In the process, they pinned down the German 91st Division and attracted the only important counterattack mounted against the Americans on D-Day. The Germans attacking the lightly armed men holding the bridgehead over the Merderet at La Fiere–Cauquiny were led by armor; fortunately, they had obsolete French tanks, which could not resist American bazookas.

At the other end of the beachhead the 8,000 men of the British 6th Airborne Division had a much better drop, despite heavy flak. Half-a-dozen glider loads, followed by a paratroop battalion, grabbed and held the crucial bridges; they smashed a gunboat that came to see what was going on, and PIAT fire drove away tanks that came to counterattack. The formidably defended Merville battery proved tougher. A whole parachute battalion was to attack it after it was blasted by 100 Lancaster bombers, while three gliders were to land right inside the German stronghold. But almost everything went wrong. Half the paratroopers were misdropped, and all five gliders carrying the paratroopers' heavy weapons broke their towropes over the Channel. Only 150 men could be collected to strike from the outside, while the glider attack on the German position went awry. The pilots of the glider tugs could not find the target, and the paratroopers had nothing to signal them with; only one glider landed nearby. The paratroopers attacked on their own. Half were killed or wounded, but they overcame the 180 defenders—only to find that instead of four deadly 150 mm. guns, the battery consisted of old 75 mm. weapons, which could not hurt the landings. The British withdrew, thinking that they had wrecked the guns—but the Germans, reoccupying the position, found that they had not! The Germans held the Merville site till July. . . .

American Troops Invade the Beaches

Meanwhile, on Utah beach, the Americans had the easiest landing on D-Day. Here the landing area was relatively sheltered and the water was calmer than off the beaches farther east. The German defenses were relatively weaker and the preliminary bombardment went well. Here, 276 Marauders from the Ninth Air Force, flying under the cloud blanket, were able to bomb visually. They largely wrecked strongpoint W5, the center of German resistance on Utah, though the Germans stubbornly defended what was left of it. A lucky accident caused the Americans to land 2,000 yards farther south than planned at a point less well defended than their original target. In a wise decision, the DD tanks were launched from less than two miles out, instead of four as planned. Almost all rolled ashore, alongside the first infantrymen from the 4th Division. The beachhead was quickly secured.

At Pointe du Hoc, between Utah and Omaha, the 2nd Ranger Battalion was to deal with a critically important shore battery. To get at it, the Rangers had to climb a cliff. They were to climb ladders borrowed from the London Fire Department, carried by DUKW amphibious trucks. But the DUKWs could not get up the beach. Covered by fire from destroyers, the Rangers went up on rocket-launched ropes instead, only to find the battery position empty. Inland, they found four of the 155 mm. guns that were supposed to be at Pointe du Hoc. The guns covered Utah beach—but had been left unmanned.

The American assault on Omaha beach proved the opposite of the experience at Utah. Practically everything went wrong, and they were up against much better defenders holding more formidable terrain. Omaha was an easy place for landing craft to run ashore, but had nothing else to recommend it. It sloped gently up to an embankment of loose stones or "shingle," often impassable even to caterpillar tracks. A seawall ran partway along the beach on the inland side of the shingle; elsewhere it was backed by sand dunes. Overlooking the beach were bluffs a hundred feet or more high, penetrated by five "draws." Four of these carried dirt roads that ultimately connected with the Norman

Allied forces land on the beach at Normandy under heavy machine-gun fire on June 6, 1944.

coastal highway, the other a trail that engineers could fix up to carry vehicles. All these draws were mined and blocked by tank traps and covered by strongpoints on the beach side. On the inland side they led to villages, which could make formidable defensive positions themselves. Omaha was believed to be defended by the underrated static 716th Division. But, as some intelligence men had suspected, it was actually manned by two regiments of the much better 352nd Division. As [American historian] Samuel Eliot Morison wrote, the Germans at Omaha had contrived "the best imitation of hell for an invading force that American troops had encountered anywhere.". . .

The surviving American infantrymen, exhausted, shocked, and disorganized, caught their breath. A few officers and natural leaders gradually rallied them. Colonel George Taylor, commander of the 1st Division's 16th Infantry Regiment, roused the men around him, shouting that "Two kinds of people are staying on this beach—the dead, and those who are going to die—now let's get the hell out of here!" It was fortunate that half the men on Omaha beach belonged to the 1st Division, the most experienced in the U.S. Army. Realizing the near-disaster ashore, destroyers closed in to shoot at the enemy strongpoints, their keels scraping the bottom. With their help, the soldiers gradually found their way up the bluffs and outflanked the defenses of the beach exits. By late morning, the Americans had recovered somewhat; and by the end of the day, most of the troops scheduled to come ashore had actually arrived. The beach was still under artillery fire, and little artillery or ammunition had gotten ashore, but the Americans were past the danger point.

British and Canadian Troops Encounter Fewer Problems

East of them, the British and Canadians had a somewhat easier time. They were up against easier terrain, held by the 716th Division, and were helped by specialized armor. Fewer machine guns bore on the beach. Nowhere was there a question of the Allies being stopped. Nevertheless, the attack was far from bloodless. The complex landing plan broke down, and the 50th Infantry Division ran into extremely tough opposition at a strongpoint at Le Hamel. Its DD tanks landed behind, instead of ahead of the specialized tanks. Nevertheless, it pushed six miles inland. Farther east, I Corps was delayed getting ashore. The Canadians encountered rocky ledges offshore, and the water was rougher. Many landing craft ran into obstacles when trying to back off the beach, and the infantry got ashore ahead of the tanks. Difficulties in clearing obstacles and opening the beach exits slowed a move inland. The Canadians' losses were heavy, but they struck deeper inland than any other seaborne element on D-Day.

The 3rd British Division, at Sword beach, had an easier time getting ashore, but also had the most formidable inland objectives allotted to any division on D-Day. It was supposed to capture a large city, Caen, which controlled the main route by which the Germans could approach the beachhead. Taking Caen would give the Allies control of the crossings of the Orne and Odon rivers. . . . [By the time the attack was over] the Germans had, however, postponed the fall of Caen for a month.

A Hard-Earned Victory

At the cost of 9,000 killed and wounded, D-Day had been a success. Henceforth, there was probably no serious chance of the Allies being pushed into the sea, even if some Germans would long cling to illusions on that score. Given the Germans' strength and dispositions on D-Day, they probably would have had little chance of entirely defeating the invasion, but might easily have done better than they did had they reacted faster. And there had been a near-catastrophe on Omaha. The bad weather, the misfired preparatory bombardments (whose failure was largely due to the weather), and a poor tactical plan that sent the American soldiers too directly against the heaviest defenses, all bore part of the blame. So did the decision to reject the specialized armor offered by the British or the amtracks and amtanks . . . in favor of the DD tanks, whose inadequacies were heightened by a failure to realize their limitations and senseless decisions on the spot. The heavy bombers should either have flown much lower, or not at all. An odd omission on D-Day, which would have startled those participating in Pacific landings, has not often been noted. There, fighter bombers and other carrier-based planes went in right ahead of the first waves, strafing and bombing just ahead of the touchdown. But there was apparently nothing like this on D-Day.

A War Correspondent's Account of D Day

Richard L. Strout

Richard L. Strout was a staff correspondent for the *Christian Science Monitor* during World War II. In the following selection, he provides a detailed account of D day, an event he witnessed from the USS *Quincy*, a heavy cruiser that departed from England on June 5. He describes the crew's preparations for the June 6 attack, followed by the bombardment of the beach as the Allies arrive onshore. He concludes that the Allies' success in establishing a beachhead guaranteed their victory in the war.

Strout died in 1990 after more than six decades as a journalist. He was awarded the Pulitzer Prize in 1978 for lifetime achievement.

O n board the heavy cruiser U.S.S. *Quincy* off France, June 7, 1944—This is a round-by-round story of the invasion of France and the opening of the Second Front.[1]

It covers the secret passage of the invasion fleet under fire and the most glorious sight of the arrival by glider of 10,000 airborne troops.

The battle continues as this is written.

The ship jolts with the explosion of shells.

But one thing is certain. Our beachhead is established.

The degree of organization disclosed is so amazing as to augur [Adolf] Hitler's overthrow.

The story begins on the open bridge of a United States heavy cruiser (the U.S.S. *Quincy*), Capt. Elliott M. Senn, United States Navy, commanding.

1. The Second Front was Western Europe (the First Front was the Soviet Union).

Richard L. Strout, "Shot-by-Shot Story of D Day," *Typewriter Battalion: Dramatic Frontline Dispatches from World War II*, edited by Jack Stenbuck. New York: William Morrow and Company, 1995. Copyright © 1995 by William Morrow and Company, Inc. Reproduced by permission.

A Seat for History's Greatest Show

It is 2 P.M. Monday, June 5. I am standing under the sky. I am dictating this story as it happens.

We have just left our anchorage. We are headed almost due east in a single line of capital ships flanked by outriders. History hangs on the weather.

On our left are the cliffs of England. We are in an Anglo-American task force. The ships' names mingle like a chant. Those of the British have come down through history. The American names sing of the New World.

Our vessel, with its home port at Boston, is one of the fleet's newest and finest. There is another task force. The combined flotilla with landing craft will be vast. There are French, Dutch and Norwegian ships.

Already, another convoy is visible carrying its own barrage balloons.

The sky is overcast. The sea is lead-colored but quiet. There is hardly any wind. Even a squall no worse than last night's would hamper landing craft, result in thousands of casualties, maybe upset the whole show. Well, we have done what we can— the weather is nature's business.

This high, open bridge covers three sides. Forward and below are three decks and gun turrets. The biggest turrets carry triple sticks of long range, dangerous-looking guns.

The prow comes to a razor edge. Like most of man's weapons, this appears beautiful. It is slim as a race horse, rhythmic as a poem.

It is so new that 1,000 of its crew are green. They speak every American accent. This spot is a magnificent grandstand seat for history's greatest show.

The Great Adventure Begins

5 P.M. We have overtaken and are passing the landing craft fleet formerly seen on the horizon. They make slow headway; their barrage balloons tied front and stern of larger craft tug ahead as though pulling.

These craft are chock-full of assault troops and supplies. They will catch up to us as we anchor in the night.

6 P.M. We have hoisted a fresh, clean battle flag. It will fly there till the engagement is over. Blue-coated figures in steel helmets are sweeping the sky and sea around me, chanting observations like football quarterbacks.

The air is tense and the men are consciously trying to break the suspense by horseplay. This has gone on for weeks. Our ship has known its mission and has been sealed. Now it is coming. The gun crew is skipping rope.

We are leaving England. The great adventure begins. The coastline fades as we steam slowly. Right under the haze close to the distant shore is another line of vessels, alternating big and little ones, moving our way stealthily under the shore line.

We look and wonder. Something marvelous is going on. All the world's ships seem to be going our way.

Rumors fly about. Yesterday, at the peak of uncertainty, came the radio news that a New York press association had falsely reported the invasion already under way. I have been asked dozens of times if this kills the whole thing.

7 P.M. A voice breaks the silence over the loudspeaker system. A battle message has been received for this task force.

"I will read it," says the voice. It is terse, pungent, without false heroics.

"Let's put the Navy ball over for a touchdown," it concludes. The sailors chuckle.

And now the chaplain offers the final prayer before the battle. All over the ship, out here in the breeze and down in the engine room beneath the surface of the sea, the men pause with bared heads.

The voice goes over the ship and into the evening air: "Our help is in the Lord."

"Ask and it shall be given, seek and ye shall find," the solemn voice concludes.

8:30 P.M. Zero hour tomorrow is 6:30. There will be general quarters tonight (which means battle stations) from 10:30.

That is the loudspeaker announcement. A hush falls on the crew, only two hours before night and day watches set in, with compartments sealed watertight.

Hurried last minute preparations are made. I walk through the compact crew compartments. Some men sit by themselves, others write letters home, some are on bunks in the canvas tiers. The voices are cheerful.

I turn in for a final nap.

10:30 P.M. The boatswain just piped, followed by the electrifying cry, "All hands man your battle stations!" Now the bugle blows "general quarters."

The sky is overcast. Somewhere up there the moon is one night from being full. Behind us are a few red streaks of sunset. Will this thick cloud conceal us? Is it possible German planes haven't spotted these great ship lines? All afternoon the number has been swelling. But the enemy has given no sign.

D-Day Arrives

Midnight. It is June 6, D-day.

The breeze has freshened. France is off ahead. There is a spurt of distant tracer bullets and a failing meteor that is really a falling airplane.

There is a gray light and we can see one another. We keep peering out, wondering when the enemy will go into action, but nothing happens.

Here is a wonderful thing: Out here in the open Channel we are following mine-swept safety lanes clearly marked so even a landsman can read them, for there are little pinpricks of buoys. Nothing that has happened has so given me the sense of extraordinary preparation.

We steam slowly. Our ship is flanked by shadowy destroyers. Only occasionally does a muffled signal flash and even on ship in the corridors, there are only his red battle lights. Now and then there is a hint of moon in the cloud blanket.

1 A.M. For an hour, airplanes have gone over us. Occasional star shells fall off there in France. Once, the moon glowed out and cast us in full relief and a silvery patch. As I dictate this, suddenly a batch of lights twinkles like July 4 sparklers. Anti-aircraft stuff! Now it is gone.

I keep thinking of home. It's 7 P.M. there now. The family is just finishing supper. It's the same in millions of American homes, children doing homework, mothers at dishes, fathers reading papers. And here we are on the dark sea moving at half speed toward history.

2 A.M. France is just over there twelve miles off. There must be hundreds of ships around us. It is impossible to see. I couldn't have believed we would get so far undetected. The Germans must know we are here. But nothing happens. Just bombers.

A few minutes ago a great flock came back from France flying low and scudding past like bats showing the prearranged signal of friends.

Behind tiny wedges come stragglers, some with limping motors. Again and again the lights blaze on the French coast. The moon dodges in and out.

Something extraordinary in bombing must be going on. When I was a child, I could see the distant glow of fireworks at Coney Island. This is like that. Just as I dictate, a fountain of sparklers sprays upward—dotted lines of tracer bullets shoot out. This must seem pretty bad on shore, but they don't know what's to come.

Arriving in France

3 A.M. We have arrived. And the slower landing craft meet us here. Then we go in with them to six miles offshore.

There will be simultaneous attacks by the Americans and British. Our beachhead is the one farthest north, the one nearest Cherbourg.

Here on the open bridge I hear the order, "Be ready to fire."

It just doesn't seem possible they don't see us. If they do, why don't they fire?

This must be the greatest concentration of bombing in the war. Everything is going off. We strain to read its meaning.

The only thing we know is that we are in Act 2.

Our performance is to reverse Dunkerque.[2]

4 A.M. Well, this is the most spectacular bombing display of all. This must be the commotion kicked up by our parachute landings.

As I write, the roar of planes is like an express train going over a viaduct. I dictate this to Chief Yeoman Charles Kidder. As I speak now, flares blaze out in fifteen to twenty clusters. I can read my watch. Flames still drop. They coil out long wriggling trails of white smoke. The water seems jet. I am so wrought up I can hardly hold still. The tension on the ship is reaching a peak.

We are going inshore. The bombs on land are so near and so big I feel the concussions. Our big guns are trained ahead.

Everybody is tense for the shore battery which does not come.

The moon is gone and it is darker than it has been. We are getting an acrid smell of torn-up soil. The eerie flares have gone out.

Well, here we go!

---

2. Also known as Dunkirk, this French seaport was the site of an Allied evacuation in late May and early June 1940. Germany had attacked the city after British, French, and Belgian troops had retreated from Belgium and headed toward Dunkerque, following Germany's conquest of Belgium. Between late May and June 4, more than 800 vessels led an evacuation of approximately 338,000 Allied troops from Dunkerque to England.

4:50 A.M. We are a few miles offshore. And no comment from the enemy. More fireworks stuff. I never imagined anything like it. The most horrible thing was two falling planes—ours, I suppose—that crashed down with great bubbling bursts of oily flames when they hit.

All nine big guns are pointed at the beach. It's getting lighter. There are yellow streaks in the cloud blanket.

5:30 A.M. It's come!

Bombardment

This is the bombardment. My ears pound. Our big guns are just under me and every time they go off—as just then—I jump and the ship jolts.

We all have cotton in our ears, but it is noisy just the same and we feel the hot blast on our faces.

We crouched behind the rail for the first one and are bolder now. We will pound the beach for an hour, picking up where the bombers quit.

Enemy shore batteries are ineffectual so far. They produce only geysers of water.

I hear the crunch of our neighbors' big guns. We all are pounding away for miles off the coast.

Here is the picture:

Dawn is breaking. There's more light every second. The sea is calm as a lake. The sky is mostly overcast.

By moving around the semi-circular bridge, I can see two-thirds of the horizon. We are in a sort of bay. We have moved in and the landing craft are coming in.

Dawn found us on Germany's doorstep like the milk bottle.

The big ship to our left is firing tracers and they go in like pitched baseballs.

The whole bowl of sky echoes with our din. While we are concerned mostly with our own beach, we see tracers from other ships zipping ashore, see the flame from guns and a few seconds later, get the report.

I can see the flag waving at our mast and the long streaks of sun-touched cloud are like its stripes.

6 A.M. We bang away regularly like a thunderbolt worked by clockwork. The individual drama goes on all around. Somehow I never imagined it would be like this.

I thought it would be all a motion picture close-up. Actually, the immensity of sky and land dwarfs everything and you have to strain at the binoculars to see what is going on. I guess that is true of all battles.

If you are right in them, you can't figure what is happening.

But here are details:

An airplane laying a smoke screen for the landing just crashed. It looked as though it was hit in midair.

We are smashing in salvos at specific objectives and every time the guns go off the whole ship jumps and so do I.

A sound like milk cans is the shells being ejected from the five-inch batteries.

Our third salvo seems to have silenced one shore battery and we have moved to the next.

Hitting the Beaches

Now at 6:30 the landing craft should be hitting the beaches.

It is H-hour.

7 A.M. An American destroyer has been hit. It is heartbreaking to watch. The enemy fire splashes again and again. We shift our guns to knock off a battery.

A whaleboat leaves the destroyer.

Distress signals blink. A cloud of steam or smoke appears. A sister ship moves in right under the fire to pick up survivors.

Forty-five minutes later, the same din, the same animated scene.

A line of ships goes ashore. And empties are coming back.

A little French village with a spire nestles at the cliffs that look so like England across the Channel.

The drama has shifted from ship to harbor.

Things probably are moving fast, but it seems amazingly slow.

8 A.M. The sun shines gloriously. This probably is the best weather ever picked for an invasion—cloudy at night, bright by day now.

Our destroyers are practically walking on the beach, blazing into the cliffs as they move. We get radio word that one emplacement in concrete and the destroyer can't rack it. Our turrets sweep around.

Bang they go! Now a second time!

It is almost impossible to stand still, so great is the will to urge that long new line of invasion barges forward. Any one of the runny little amphibious beetles makes a story in itself.

It is like picking a particular ant.

Here in my binoculars I see an ugly squarish little craft making for shore with a lace of foam in front. It reaches the beach, the white disappears, it waddles up. I can't see, but its guns are probably going.

On the sands are hulks of other boats—motionless. They have hit mines.

9 A.M. No sleep—and a plate of beans for breakfast. It seems as though it must be afternoon.

Our radio has just picked up a German radiocast denying any troops are ashore. They seem thoroughly befuddled.

They say we made an attempt at Dunkerque and Le Havre.[3] It seems a complete surprise.

Noon. Everything depends on speed. We have a landing, but we had that at Dieppe.[4] Can we stick and can we go in fast enough to pinch off Cherbourg?

The whole drama is that line of ships. What it looks like is an ant line.

One line moves an army with crumbs and another returns to the crust. Here they are moving like that—little black ships, but all sizes.

A big one with a whole rear end that unfolds on the beach or a little one with a truck or two. They are all pretty squat and ugly—and the most beautiful sight I ever saw.

Yet it looks so quiet and peaceful. The splashes of water look like top splashes. Except when the splashes come in our direction.

There is one persistent battery that keeps trying to get us. It quiets after we fire and then comes on again after we shift to something else.

One earlier target we got in the first salvo.

Listening to the Battle

2 P.M. I have just had on the head phones in the communications room. Shore groups with walkie-talkies are telling the parent control what they find.

It is all in a jargon of communications nomenclature. The parent voice calls out loudly and commandingly through the static.

More and more crackling static. Suddenly a quiet voice identifies itself.

3. Le Havre is a French seaport that suffered heavy damage during World War II due to Allied bombing.   4. The French port of Dieppe was the site of a British raid in August 1942.

"I am pinned down," says the quiet voice. "I am between machine-gun and pill-box cross fire." So that's it.

And now our radio leaves him.

A station reports that "firing from the bluff is continuing." It reports that the water obstacles are being taken care of. The incoming tide is helping.

That's what a battle sounds like under the scream of shells. We can't really tell what's happening. We are in it, but we might be losing for all we know.

4 P.M. Well, things are going well. We know because we have just heard a British Broadcasting Corporation (BBC) broadcast! BBC seems delighted. It says reports are splendid. O.K. by us.

That far bluff is still spitting fire, though, and the elusive shore battery has splashed us with water. What does BBC advise?

But we are so weary now we are going to sleep on our feet anyway.

6 P.M. Six of the clumsy mechanized landing crafts (LCM's) go by—the most angular craft ever built. Their front end, that ought to be high, is low, and vice versa. Not even its mother could love it. They are like wallowing watering troughs.

They carry a five-man crew and will lug a tank ashore. They come in abreast closer than anything so far. Those six, somehow, epitomize the whole affair. I can pick out figures—almost faces—with my glasses. To the men on shore they must look like ministering angels.

I can see the burly captain and even at this distance notice his arms akimbo. He is contemptuously looking at our towering warship and staring it out of counterance.

Then he sweeps the battle with uncomplimentary eye—the very image of a Hudson River tugboat captain. If I talked to him, I bet he would have a tough Jersey accent and would take backtalk from nobody, see—not from the Germans, nor from a warship.

We let go an eight-inch gun salvo over his right ear that must at least establish a feeling of joint respect.

All the time I have been typing, the ship has been blasting ahead. The typewriter jumps with the jolt.

Midnight. We are, I think, winning the battle. And here is the place to stop because I have just seen the most glorious sight of all. The paratroopers have come in. It was a scene of almost unbelievable romance and it probably revolutionizes warfare.

Right out of the east came suddenly a bigger and bigger roar of sound, as if all the planes in England were droning, and then here appeared line on line of big bombers, each towing a glider.

They curved over us in a mighty crescent and sped over the shore into the sunset.

Then, as the first batch passed and the second appeared, the bombers of the first were coming back again singly, this time having released their gliders filled with crack troops to reinforce the weary invasion companies that have battled all day.

Just at 11 o'clock, a new batch, even bigger than before, skimmed over in the late dusk of double summer time. They were so close you could see the rope that bound plane and glider taut as a fiddle string—all in perfect formation.

In each of the three earlier flights, there were many planes and as many gliders. Just now there are even more.

It was a fantasy out of the future.

Last week, when correspondents on the battle fleet were briefed, we were told something about airborne troops. It seemed fantastic—the number was so large. But I am beginning to believe it.

What a sight that overhead reinforcement must have been to the muddy, blackened men below. It had the dash and elan of a cavalry charge.

After seeing the things I have in the past twenty-four hours, I know one thing—the road may be tough, but we can't lose.

American Soldiers Recall Their Haunting Experiences at Dachau

by Flint Whitlock

When American troops liberated Dachau on April 29, 1945, they made chilling discoveries that forever redefined the world's understanding of inhumanity. Of the Nazis' two thousand labor and extermination camps, Dachau had been the first. When Theodor Eicke became the inspector general for all camps, he used Dachau as his model. His purpose was to establish an institution that would terrify potential opposition to the Nazi regime. Dachau was used frequently to train the SS (the harsh security team used to exert authority in Nazi-occupied territories) to treat prisoners as nonhumans and to kill without remorse. SS members were not the only ones to practice cruelty at Dachau; Nazi scientists performed brutal experiments on prisoners there.

Beginning in 1938, Dachau was the destination of most prisoners captured in countries invaded by Germany. When the camp was liberated, its prisoners represented more than thirty nationalities. Although Dachau did not exterminate inmates with gas (the chambers were built in 1942 but were never used), tens of thousands of pris-

Flint Whitlock, "Liberating Dachau," *World War II*, vol. 14, March 2000, p. 26. Copyright © 2000 by Primedia Special Interest Publications. Reproduced by permission.

oners were tortured and executed there or died of illness, and many more were sent to camps that used gas chambers. In early 1945, the already inhumane conditions at Dachau worsened when other camps sent their prisoners to Dachau when they evacuated during the Allied advance; the overcrowding became unbearable. Reports indicate that as many as sixteen hundred people were housed in quarters designed for two hundred. The prisoners' poor health, combined with cramped quarters and unsanitary conditions, made them vulnerable to illness. Between one hundred and two hundred prisoners died every day from typhoid.

When American troops found the camp, more than thirty thousand prisoners were liberated. Most of the SS guards had left, taking seven thousand prisoners on a death march. The remaining guards were subject to the horror and outrage of the prisoners and the soldiers involved in the liberation. The outrage felt by the soldiers foretells the visceral reaction of the American people.

In addition to his frequent contributions to *World War II* magazine, Flint Whitlock is the coauthor of *Soldiers on Skis: A Pictorial Memoir of the 10th Mountain Division* and the author of *The Rock of Anzio: From Sicily to Dachau: A History of the Forty-Fifth Infantry Division.*

I n March 1945, as the Allied armies were squeezing Germany from the east and west, the Germans were either trying frantically to evacuate the concentration and death camps and hide the evidence or making last-ditch efforts to exterminate as many Jews and other political prisoners as possible before the Reich was defeated.

Because of reports from escapees, Lt. Gen. Wade H. Haislip's advancing XV Corps (consisting of the 3rd, 42nd, 45th and 86th Infantry divisions, the 20th Armored Division and the 106th Cavalry Group, all heading for Munich) was prepared to deal with horrific conditions when it reached Dachau at the end of April.

Much had already been learned about what had gone on at concentration camps after Buchenwald—some 220 miles north of Dachau—had been discovered by the U.S. 6th Armored Division on April 11. The unanswered questions were: How many—if any—of the camp's inmates would still be alive and which unit would liberate the camp? It was the latter question that would fuel the flames of an interdivisional dispute between veterans of the 45th and 42nd Infantry divisions that continues to this day.

Poring over maps, officers at XV Corps headquarters saw that the 45th was in the best position to reach Dachau first. On April 28, a call was made to Maj. Gen. Robert T. Frederick, former commander of the elite 1st Special Service Force and now commanding general of the war-weary 45th "Thunderbird" Division, setting the wheels in motion for the 45th to liberate Dachau.

The 45th had already seen more than 500 days of combat—including four amphibious assaults, months of brutal warfare in the snowy mountains of Italy, the saving of both the Salerno and Anzio beachheads, and the punishing drive through German-occupied France and the Siegfried Line. When Lt. Col. Felix Sparks, commanding the 3rd Battalion, 157th Infantry Regiment, 45th Infantry Division, received orders diverting him from the drive on Munich to the liberation of KL Dachau, he was not happy. He felt the change of orders would slow his battalion down. "I didn't consider the concentration camp a military objective," he said.

The message to Sparks read, "Dachau may be very important, both militarily and politically. Be especially careful of operations in this sector." At 0922 hours on the 29th, Sparks received another message: "Upon capture of Dachau by any battalion, post air-tight guard and allow no one to enter or leave."

Sparks was also told that, once the camp was secured, nothing was to be disturbed. The evidence of atrocities was to be left for an international prisoners committee to investigate. Most of the men of the 157th knew little or nothing about concentration camps and had no idea what these orders meant or what lay ahead. They received a grim education on the unseasonably cold day of Sunday, April 29, as they cautiously advanced through the town, looking for snipers. All was unnervingly silent. In the center of the city, Sparks' men came to an intact railroad bridge and crossed the river, then followed a set of tracks that led toward the southwestern corner of the SS complex about one kilometer away. The time was approximately 1215.

The Company Encounters Horror

"We went along the south side of the camp and I saw the main entrance and decided to avoid it; if the Germans were going to defend it, I figured that's where they'd do it," Colonel Sparks later said. "So we found a railroad track that went into the camp on the southwest side." Sparks' decision to avoid approaching the main gate would result in much confusion and controversy for decades to come. Inside that main gate, the Germans had been waiting, ready to surrender.

Sparks conferred briefly with 1st Lt. William P. Walsh, commanding officer of I Company, the battalion's lead element. Sparks told Walsh his orders were to seize the camp, seal it and let no one in or out.

The men of I Company moved out, unprepared for what they were about to encounter. Between the town and the camp, the Thunderbirds saw a string of 39 boxcars and open gondola cars standing on the track. If ever the American soldier needed confirmation as to why he was at war, why he was required to put his life on the line day after day, it was contained in those 39 railroad cars.

As the GIs cautiously approached the boxcars, the sickening stench of death grew ever stronger. In each railroad car were piles of rotting human corpses—a total of 2,310 men, women and children—either totally naked or partially clad in blue-and-white-striped concentration camp uniforms. Most of them had starved to death while being evacuated from Buchenwald 22 days earlier in an effort to keep them from falling into the hands of the approaching Allies. A few with enough strength to attempt escape had been shot down by the SS guards or brutally beaten with rifle butts.

The Soldiers' Reactions to the Corpses

Private First Class John Lee was one of the first men on the scene. "Most of the GIs just stood there in silence and disbelief," he later remembered. "We had seen men in battle blown apart, burnt to death and die many different ways, but we were never prepared for this. Several of the dead lay there with their eyes open. It seemed they were looking at us and saying, 'What took you so long?'"

To a man, I Company was seething with anger at what they had discovered on the railroad tracks. "Tears were in everyone's eyes from the sight and smell," Lee recalled. "Suddenly, GIs started swearing and crying with such rage and remarked, 'Let's kill every one of those bastards,' and 'Don't take any SS alive!'

Never had I seen men so fighting mad willing to throw caution to the wind."

I Company continued grimly on, many of the men stunned and sickened at what they had encountered, others bent on avenging the mass killing. Suddenly, four SS men, their hands held high, emerged from a hiding place and tried to surrender to Walsh's party. But Walsh was not having it. He had heard stories of the notorious SS atrocities, and he had just seen firsthand the awful fruits of their labor. Filled with rage, Walsh herded the four men into one of the railroad cars and emptied his pistol into them. They were lying there moaning when Private Albert Pruitt came up and finished them off with his rifle.

Liberators and Prisoners Become Violent

The killing of unarmed German POWs did not trouble many of the men in I Company that day. Lieutenant Harold Moyer, a platoon commander in I Company, later testified: "I heard every man, or a lot of men, who said we should take no prisoners. I felt the same way myself. I believe every man in the outfit who saw those boxcars prior to the entrance to Dachau felt he was justified in meting out death as a punishment to the Germans who were responsible."

As I Company neared the SS infirmary, Private Lee recalled: "My buddy and I heard a loud scream and commotion around the side of one of the buildings. We went to investigate and there were two inmates beating a [German] medic in a white coat with shovels. By the time we got there, he was a bloody mess. We ordered them to halt. They said they were Poles, and one of them dropped his pants to show he had been castrated in the hospital and this German was somehow involved in the operation."

Near the camp's infirmary, Walsh's men were rounding up a number of German soldiers and separating the SS men from the ordinary Wehrmacht troops. The SS men were then herded into a large, enclosed area and lined up against a high stucco wall that formed part of a coal yard for the camp's nearby power plant.

Several of the SS prisoners in the coal yard refused to keep their hands up, and others began muttering to each other in German. At that point, the handful of GIs guarding them were getting nervous. Lee recalled that the GIs "shouted for the SS to keep their Goddamned hands up and stay back."

Lieutenant Walsh ordered the others to set up a machine gun

facing the prisoners and to fire if they didn't stay back. The gunner, Private William C. Curtin, loaded the belt in the machine gun and pulled back on the cocking lever so the gun would be ready to fire if necessary. The SS men, seeing the machine gun being cocked, apparently thought they were about to be shot. They panicked and started toward the Americans. Someone yelled "Fire!" and the machine gun opened up with a short burst of fire. Three or four riflemen also fired.

Shortly before the firing began, Sparks, who had been observing the roundup of Germans in the coal yard, had been distracted by a soldier approaching him. Sparks recalled: "He said, 'Colonel, you should see what we found,' so I started to go off with him. I hadn't gotten more than 10 yards away when all of a sudden the machine gun opened up. I wheeled around. The gunner had fired one burst—maybe 10 or 12 shots—at the guards." The SS guards dived for the ground, but in the hail of gunfire, 17 of them were killed. Sparks said: "I ran back and kicked the gunner in the back and knocked him forward onto the gun, then grabbed him by the collar and yelled, 'What the hell are you doing?' He said they were trying to get away, and then he started crying. I pulled out my .45 and fired several shots into the air and said there would be no more firing unless I gave the order. I told them I was taking over command of the company."

Sparks said: "I never like to see people killed unnecessarily, no matter what they have done. We did kill some people there that I consider [were killed] unnecessarily. However, given the circumstances, well, I'm sorry about it. It was just one of those things that no one could control. We tried to take prisoners and treat them honorably. But that was one situation that I was just unable to control for a short time.

The Discovery of the Crematorium

Inwardly boiling at what had just taken place but understanding the motivation behind the troops' actions, Sparks directed that the wounded men should be taken to the infirmary, then remembered the enlisted man who had wanted to show him what new horrors I Company had uncovered. Sparks soon arrived at the crematorium, where he saw piles of emaciated corpses, stacked nearly to the ceiling. A count later revealed approximately 200 bodies.

The corpses found there and throughout the camp, including the bodies of the SS men in the coal yard, were left undisturbed for several days while investigators did their work and photographers recorded the scene. A stunned Corporal James Bird later came upon the horrors in the crematorium. After that experience, he found that his mind was forever etched with nightmarish images. "I recall seeing the ovens used to burn bodies and recollect there were still some partly consumed bodies in some of them," Bird said. "One of my buddies photographed many scenes there, and later provided us with copies. I do not have them now because I think my mother destroyed them, since they were beyond her belief."

By now, I Company was only a few yards from the northwest corner of the prison compound. At least 31,000 inmates were huddled in the barracks there, not knowing if the next few minutes would bring liberation or death. Many feared that as the Americans neared, the SS men would carry out Reichsfuhrer Heinrich Himmler's orders to dispose of them all.

The 42nd Infantry Division Arrives

Unknown to Sparks, a small advance party from the U.S. Army's 42nd "Rainbow" Infantry Division was rapidly closing in on the camp from the south at that point. As with all of the other American units dashing through Bavaria, the prize those GIs had in view was Munich. At 0220 hours on the 29th, the 42nd's commander, Maj. Gen. Harry J. Collins, sent a message to his 222nd Infantry Regiment: "Combat battalion to be moved as soon as possible, regiment to follow thereafter as desired, Case of champagne to first battalion to enter Munich." Collins made no mention of Dachau because he knew his division had not been authorized by the Seventh Army to attempt entering KL Dachau—that was the 45th's assignment. But a contingent of American and foreign war correspondents had heard the 42nd was close to the camp and were evidently pressing the division to move toward it—and take them along. There were also the humanitarian concerns. How could he say no? He ordered Brig. Gen. Henning Linden, the assistant division commander, to take a small patrol into the camp.

According to Linden's later testimony to the inspector general, at approximately 1530 the 42nd's advance party, following on the heels of the 45th, came upon the ghastly scene at the railroad siding. Technician Fifth Grade John R. Veitch, who was driving a jeep, recalled: "I had no idea where we were going or what we were going to see. Then we encountered the train with all the bodies. It was terrible."

Linden's party entered the camp at the railroad gate, then turned east toward the main gate. Leading the group were two generals—Linden and Brig. Gen. Charles Y. Banfill, deputy commander for operations, U.S. Eighth Air Force, who was accompanying the 42nd to observe the effects of supporting aerial operations. Others in the entourage included three junior officers and a number of enlisted drivers and bodyguards. Two jeeps carrying members of the press also tagged along, with a Belgian reporter and a photographer in one and Sergeant Peter Furst, a writer with *Stars and Stripes,* and war correspondent Marguerite Higgins in the other.

Higgins was a 25-year-old [*sic*] fledgling war reporter from the *New York Herald Tribune* who had been in Europe only since March but was determined to make a name for herself. Two weeks earlier, at Buchenwald, she had received a quick introduction to the horrors of the SS camps. But Buchenwald was yesterday's news. Higgins wanted to be in on the liberation of a camp. While at Buchenwald, she teamed up with Furst, who had a jeep, and the two of them pressed forward toward Dachau along the same general route used by the 45th and 42nd divisions. Furst and Higgins arrived at the main gate about the same time as Linden's party.

The 42nd Infantry Division Accepts the Camp's Surrender

John Veitch recalled, "We got to the outskirts of the camp and heard a lot of small-arms fire," Not knowing if enemy fire was being directed at them, Linden's party, along with Furst and Higgins, scrambled out the jeeps and took cover in a drainage ditch near the camp's main gate. "The small-arms fire letup. The firing was coming from the 45th, already inside the camp, and then, out of the gate area, came this SS officer. I think there was another man with him. I ended up going up to this SS officer and stuck my .45 in his ribs and told him to put his hands on his head. I'm hitting him in the ribs, trying to get his hands up, but he saw I was just a GI and he was an officer. I brought him back to the general and Linden said to me, 'Tell him to put his hands up.' I said, 'Sir, he won't do it.' Well, General Linden always carried a little stick, kind of a hickory stick with a knob on the end, and he hauled off and hit this guy up the side of the head and said, 'Put your hands up' and he immediately did. He saw that Linden was a general officer."

A brief surrender ceremony took place near the main gate, with the German detachment under the protection of a white flag on a broomstick held by Victor Maurer, a Swiss Red Cross representative. Unaware that the 45th had arrived at Dachau first and was, at that very moment, clearing out the SS camp's buildings, SS Untersturmfuhrer Heinrich Wicker officially surrendered the camp to the 42nd, thereby fueling a debate between the two divisions that lasts to this day regarding which was the true liberator of Dachau. . . .

Members of the 42nd Enter the Camp

Meanwhile, at the main gate, Linden and the small knot of Rainbowmen were champing at the bit. They had heard sporadic gunshots and were anxiously waiting to enter the camp. At last a jeep with Lt. Col. Lucien Buldoc in it roared into view. It was decided to send Lieutenant Cowling on another scouting mission inside the camp. Cowling, possibly accompanied by an enlisted man, moved in cautiously. He went about two blocks north, then turned east and discovered the Jourhaus gate 150 yards ahead of him. Seeing a crowd of inmates beginning to form at the Jourhaus, Cowling tried to tell them help was on the way. He then returned to Linden's group at the main gate and told them to come see what he had found.

The advance party from the 42nd Division arrived at the Jourhaus, where a group of SS guards emerged and surrendered to Linden's men without incident. In his testimony to the assistant inspector general, Linden said: "I moved in with my guards into [the military part of the camp], and I found the inmates—having seen the American uniform of my guards there, and those of the 45th Division—approaching the main stockade [i.e., the Jourhaus and the western side of the prisoner enclosure] from the east, had stormed to the fence in riotous joy. This seething mass increased in intensity until the surge against the steel barbed-wire fence was such that it broke in several places, and inmates poured out into the roadway between the fence and the moat [canal]. In this process, several were electrocuted on the charged fence.". . .

On his way to the Jourhaus, Sparks saw prisoners streaming from their barracks by the thousands and rushing toward the wire that enclosed them. "Walking along the canal almost to the Jourhaus, I saw a large number of naked bodies stretched out along the ends of the barracks," Sparks recalled. "I estimated there were about 200 bodies there. I also spotted quite a few of my men at the Jourhaus. About this time, the camp erupted. The prisoners came out of the barracks shouting and screaming."

Thousands of inmates dashed to the wire enclosure, emitting an unearthly howl—a howl of rage at what had befallen them, and a howl of joy at their redemption. Sparks said: "I told Karl Mann, my interpreter, to yell at them and tell them that we couldn't let them out, but that food and medicine would be arriving soon. Then I saw bodies flying through the air, with the prisoners tearing at them with their hands. I had Karl ask what was going on. The prisoners told him that they were killing the informers among them. They actually tore them to pieces with their bare hands. This went on for about five minutes until they wore themselves out. I had Karl tell them to send their leaders to the fence, where I told them to keep calm, that medicine and food would be coming soon. This seemed to settle them down."

The 42nd and 45th Infantry Divisions Meet

Sparks recalled what he saw when he reached the Jourhaus: "A beautiful iron gate to the concentration camp itself . . . that had a sign on it that said in German, 'Work makes you free.' Of course, they worked those prisoners to death. I was standing there at the gate, talking to one of my officers about security when, all of a sudden, I saw three jeeps coming up and they stopped at the end of the little bridge that spanned the canal [at the Jourhaus]." In the jeeps were Generals Linden and Banfill, Colonels Bolduc and Fellenz, along with several others, including journalist Higgins and photographer Furst.

The jeeps stopped at the western end of the bridge that spanned the canal, and Sparks talked briefly with Linden. Sparks said Linden told him that Higgins wanted to enter the camp to interview the inmates. Sparks replied that his orders prohibited anyone but his men from entering the camp. Higgins then spoke up, demanding to be allowed inside the enclosure. She said, "Colonel, there are some famous people in there," and rattled off a list of names, including the deposed Austrian Chancellor Kurt von Schuschnigg with his wife and daughter, Pastor Martin Niemoller, an anti-Nazi theologian, Hitler's former chief of staff

Franz Halder—and many others.

Sparks reiterated his orders. Undeterred, Higgins ran to the gate and began to open it. She was nearly trampled by prisoners trying to get out. Sparks recalled that his men were forced to fire warning shots over the heads of the prisoners to achieve order before they could reclose the gate. "When the firing started," Sparks said, "it scared this woman and she ran back to her jeep."

At this point, a violent argument broke out between Sparks and Linden—an argument remembered clearly more than 50 years later by men from both divisions. Exactly what touched off the argument has never been conclusively determined. . . .

Liberators Are Haunted by the Experience

Many of the soldiers were thankful they had reached the camp in time to save the lives of many of the inmates, but they discovered it was virtually impossible not to be repelled by the awful conditions in the camp. Sidney C. Horn, a member of I Company, 157th, recalled the terrible overcrowding and the lack of proper sanitation: "The people wanted to hug you and love you for what you were doing, but the stench was so bad, you couldn't keep from running from them."

As the gray, sunless day settled into a cold night, a sense of relief spread within the inmates of KL Dachau. From the barracks came sounds of laughter, singing and prayers of thanksgiving. There was little joy, however, among the American liberators. Although they had undoubtedly helped save thousands of lives, many of the men of I Company felt sick and depressed over what they had seen and heard that day. For some, it was a delayed reaction.

John Lee recalled: "That night was when the realization really hit. We had to guard the bakery, our squad. No one ate chow that night . . . everyone was sick. I was sick constantly all night long. I don't think there was a guy who slept that night, and I don't think there was a guy who didn't cry openly that night." He added: "I really didn't feel good about what happened there, but also I have to admit there was a certain amount of revenge and, in a way, I felt that even though these [guards] may not have been the men who perpetrated this sort of thing, at least you paid back a little bit for these people, what happened to them. I realized you can't resolve it by doing that—it was wrong, what happened there, but you had to have been there to see what we saw."

A War Correspondent Reveals the Horrors of Dachau to American Readers

by Marguerite Higgins

In April 1945 American troops began liberating concentration camps in Germany. Among the first to bring the horrific news of the camps to the American people was Marguerite Higgins, a young war correspondent who actually accompanied troops on April 29 when they liberated Dachau. The information she related to the people back home was shocking, disturbing, and infuriating. Americans reacted strongly to the news, and to this day, the horrors that confronted the liberators of Dachau and other camps continue to shape the way Americans feel about and interpret World War II.

When she accompanied U.S. troops into Dachau, Higgins was a twenty-four-year-old war correspondent trying to make a name for herself with the *New York Herald Tribune.* She did. Her tenacity, courage, and ability to "scoop" her fellow reporters earned her acclaim and a 1945 U.S. Army combat ribbon for services above and beyond the call of duty. She went on to fulfill her early journalistic promise by becoming one of the prominent war correspondents of the Korean War and being named a co-winner of the 1951 Pulitzer Prize in international reporting. In addition to her newspaper writing, Higgins authored five books before her premature death in 1966 from a disease contracted on a tour of Vietnam, India, and Pakistan.

D achau, Germany, April 29 (delayed)—Troops of the United States 7th Army liberated 33,000 prisoners this afternoon at this first and largest of the Nazi concentration camps. Some of the prisoners had endured for eleven years the horrors of notorious Dachau.

The liberation was a frenzied scene. Inmates of the camp hugged and embraced the American troops, kissed the ground before them and carried them shoulder high around the place.

Entering the Camp

The Dachau camp, in which at least a thousand prisoners were killed last night before the S.S. (Elite Guard) men in charge fled, is a grimmer and larger edition of the similarly notorious Buchenwald camp near Weimar.

This correspondent and Peter Furst, of the army newspaper *"Stars and Stripes,"* were the first two Americans to enter the inclosure at Dachau, where persons possessing some of the best brains in Europe were held during what might have been the most fruitful years of their lives.

While a United States 45th Infantry Division patrol was still fighting a way down through S.S. barracks to the north, our jeep and two others from the 42d Infantry drove into the camp inclosure through the southern entrance. As men of the patrol with us busied themselves accepting an S.S. man's surrender, we impressed a soldier into service and drove with him to the prisoners' barracks. There he opened the gate after pushing the body of a prisoner shot last night while attempting to get out to meet the Americans.

There was not a soul in the yard when the gate was opened. As we learned later, the prisoners themselves had taken over control of their inclosure the night before, refusing to obey any further orders from the German guards, who had retreated to the outside. The prisoners maintained strict discipline among themselves, remaining close to their barracks so as not to give the S.S. men all excuse for mass murder.

But the minute the two of us entered, a jangled barrage of "Are you Americans?" in about sixteen languages came from the barracks 200 yards from the gate. An affirmative nod caused pandemonium.

Tattered, emaciated men, weeping, yelling and shouting, "Long live America!" swept toward the gate in a mob. Those who could not walk limped or crawled. In the confusion, they were so hysterically happy that they took the S.S. man for an American. During a wild five minutes he was patted on the back, paraded on shoulders and embraced enthusiastically by prisoners. The arrival of the American soldier soon straightened out the situation.

Prisoners Charge the Tower

I happened to be the first through the gate, and the first person to rush up to me turned out to be a Polish Catholic priest, a deputy of August Cardinal Hlond, Primate of Poland, who was not a little startled to discover that the helmeted, uniformed, be-goggled individual he had so heartily embraced was not a man.

In the excitement, which was not the least dampened by the German artillery, and the sounds of battle in the northern part of the camp, some of the prisoners died trying to pass through electrically charged barbed wire. Some who got out after the wires were decharged joined in the battle, when some ill-advised S.S. men holding out in a tower fired upon them.

The prisoners charged the tower and threw all six S.S. men out the window.

After an hour and a half of cheering, the crowd, which would virtually mob each soldier that dared to venture into the excited, milling group, was calmed down enough to make possible a tour of the camp. The only American prisoner, a flyer with the rank of major, took some of the soldiers through.

According to the prisoners, the most famous individuals who had been at the camp had been removed by S.S. men to Innsbrueck. Among them were Leon Blum, former French Premier, and his wife; the Rev. Martin Niemoeller, German church leader; Kurt Schuschnigg, Chancellor of Austria at the time of the anschluss (he was said to have been alive a few days ago); Gabriel Piquet, Bishop of St. Etienne; Prince Leopold of Prussia; Baron Fritz Cirini, aide of Prince Leopold; Richard Schmitz, former Mayor of Vienna, and Marshal Stalin's son, Jacob.

Starving Prisoners in Cramped Quarters

The barracks at Dachau, like those at Buchenwald, had the stench of death and sickness. But at Dachau there were six barracks like the infamous No. 61 at Buchenwald, where the starving and dying lay virtually on top of each other in quarters where 1,200 men occupied a space intended for 200. The dead—300 died of sickness yesterday—lay on concrete walks outside the quarters and others were being carried out as the reporters went through.

The mark of starvation was on all the emaciated corpses. Many of the living were so frail it seemed impossible they could still be holding on to life.

The Camp Was Designed for Torture and Killing

The crematorium and torture chambers lay outside the prisoner inclosures. Situated in a wood close by, a new building had been built by prisoners under Nazi guards. Inside, in the two rooms used as torture chambers, an estimated 1,200 bodies were piled.

In the crematorium itself were hooks on which the S.S. men hung their victims when they wished to flog them or to use any of the other torture instruments. Symbolic of the S.S. was a mural the S.S. men themselves had painted on the wall. It showed a headless man in uniform with the S.S. insigne on the collar. The man was astride a huge inflated pig, into which he was digging his spurs.

The prisoners also showed reporters the ground where men knelt and were shot in the back of the neck. On this very spot a week ago a French general, a resistance leader under General Charles de Gaulle, had been killed.

Bodies of Prisoners Are Everywhere

Just beyond the crematorium was a ditch containing some 2,000 more bodies, which had been hastily tossed there in the last few days by the S.S. men who were so busy preparing their escape they did not have time to burn the bodies.

Below the camp were cattle cars in which prisoners from Buchenwald had been transported to Dachau. Hundreds of dead were still in the cars due to the fact that prisoners in the camp had rejected S.S. orders to remove them. It was mainly the men from these cattle cars that the S.S. leaders had shot before making their escape. Among those who had been left for dead in the cattle cars was one man still alive who managed to lift himself from the heap of corpses on which he lay.

The Bombing of Hiroshima and Nagasaki:
August 6 and 9, 1945

Hiroshima and Nagasaki Ushered in the Atomic Age

by Rinjiro Sodei

On August 6, 1945, a B-29 bomber called the *Enola Gay* dropped the first atomic bomb used as a weapon. The target was the Japanese city of Hiroshima, which was engulfed in an enormous mushroom after the bomb hit. The force and heat of the bomb claimed eighty thousand lives and left thousands of people injured. The massive waves of heat set the city on fire, leaving it in ruins. Two days later, the Soviet Union declared war on Japan. The next day, August 9, the United States dropped a second bomb on Japan, this time hitting the city of Nagasaki. The second atomic bomb killed forty thousand people. On August 10 Japan announced its unconditional surrender, bringing World War II to a close.

Over the years, historians have debated the reasons Japan surrendered, but all agree that the bombings of Hiroshima and Nagasaki were major factors. The issues surrounding the bombings are still alive and well, as evidenced by the swirl of controversy surrounding a Smithsonian exhibit that was scheduled to open on the fiftieth anniversary of the bombing of Hiroshima. The original vision was sweeping, with plans to cover everything from the *Enola Gay* to the victims in the aftermath of the event. Many scholars condemned much of the text accompanying the exhibit, noting that it depicted Japan as a helpless victim of atomic warfare with no choice but to surrender. Some also criticized the portrayal of the victims and sur-

Rinjiro Sodei, "Hiroshima/Nagasaki as History and Politics," *Bulletin of Concerned Asian Scholars*, vol. 27, 1995, pp. 37–41. Copyright © 1995 by *Bulletin of Concerned Asian Scholars*. Reproduced by permission.

vivors. Historians wanted a balanced, historically objective exhibit, and they felt strongly that the Smithsonian was not moving in that direction. The outcry was so vehement that ultimately the exhibit only included the *Enola Gay*.

Another exhibit that historians criticize is the Hiroshima Peace Memorial Museum in Hiroshima. This museum houses objects recovered during the cleanup after the bomb, along with photos and stories. What are missing, claim some scholars, are the historical facts about Japan's aggression during the war. The museum, they claim, seems to suggest that Japan was the victim of the overbearing, warmongering Allies.

Japanese scholar Rinjiro Sodei addresses these two exhibits in the context of the larger issues surrounding the bombing of Japan. Sodei believes historians have a responsibility to represent the events of the past accurately and responsibly. As an educator and historian, Sodei has been involved in the Japanese Political Science Association and the Peace Studies Association of Japan. He is a professor of history and politics at Hosei University in Tokyo and the author of *Two Thousand Days of MacArthur* (1975) and *Were We the Enemy? American Survivors of Hiroshima* (1998).

There has been endless controversy concerning what really brought Japan to its knees on 14 August 1945. Was it the atomic bombing of Hiroshima on 6 August? The Soviet entry into the war two days later? Or was it not the combination of these two blows that did the job? Some even argue that the bombing of Nagasaki the day after the Soviet Union entered the war was necessary as a coup de grace. Here I would like to set aside the familiar argument of the U.S. Strategic Bombing Survey that Japan would have surrendered anyway—without the bombs, without the Soviet entry, and even without a U.S. invasion of Japan's main islands—and instead present the testimonies of three commentators from three different countries.

One is a U.S., Central Intelligence Agency (CIA) analyst whom I encountered here in Washington more than a decade ago. He volunteered that his research convinced him that it was the bomb that finished Japan. The CIA man quite naturally dismissed the Soviet entry as a significant factor.

The second commentator is a Soviet diplomat whom I interviewed in Moscow in 1982. He claimed that he personally observed the aftermath of Hiroshima within a week of the bombing. How he got there is a long story. To make a long story short, Ivan Nikolaevich Tzekhonya, a second secretary of the Soviet embassy in Tokyo, accompanied by a Japanese Foreign Office official, drove all the way to Hiroshima and wandered around the ruined city for a couple of days until he heard the emperor's radio statement of surrender when he was in the nearby city of Kure. Tzekhonya's report, including some photographs, must have been duly submitted to [Soviet leader Joseph] Stalin through Ambassador Malik, who was was in Japan. Tzekhonya's main point was that the atomic bomb was merely a bigger bomb, and its effect was less impressive than the Tokyo air raid of five months previously, which he also witnessed. In his view, Japan surrendered simply because the great Soviet Union entered the war.

The third witness, so to speak; is a Japanese Imperial Navy admiral, Hoshina Zenshiro, who was the last surviving member of the meeting at which Emperor Hirohito opted for Japan's surrender. His impression was that it was a combination of two blows that eventually brought Japan to its knees: the bombing of Hiroshima and the Soviet entry into the war. It was this quick one-two punch that knocked out Japan. Admiral Hoshina added that the Nagasaki bomb was "an appendix"—meaning, I believe, not so crucial.

Now, whom to believe? This is not a simple task, because none of these so-called witnesses were neutral. The CIA analyst obviously represented the official U.S. view: it was the atomic bombs that ended the war, period. The Soviet diplomat predictably dismissed the importance of the bombs. Most Japanese, myself included, tend to side with Admiral Hoshina in placing equal weight on the bombs and the shock of the Soviet Union's declaration of war.

The Bomb Was a Factor in the Surrender

In this context it was interesting to find in the final version of the proposed Smithsonian script a statement from Emperor Hirohito to General [Douglas] MacArthur that "the peace party did not prevail until the bombing of Hiroshima created a situation that could be dramatized." There are several versions of what the emperor told MacArthur at their first meeting on 27 September 1945, but to Japanese scholars such as myself this is totally new.

Where did such a statement come from?

In any case, in his surrender broadcast to the nation the emperor did declare that the cruelty of the new weapon forced him to surrender. This was also quoted in the original Smithsonian script: "The enemy has begun to employ a new and most cruel bomb, the power of which to do damage is indeed incalculable, taking the toll of many innocent lives. Should we continue to fight, it would not only result in an ultimate collapse and obliterating of the Japanese nation, but it would lead to the total extinction of human civilization."

Thus the war came to an end. The bomb was a factor in Japan's surrender, but not the only one. The more interesting issue, however, is whether the bombing of Hiroshima and Nagasaki was an end or a beginning. To the U.S. GIs who were awaiting the invasion of Japan's main islands, the atomic bombs certainly signaled the end of that bloody war. As for the crew of the *Enola Gay*, once their mission was accomplished they became part of history. As indicated in the Senate resolution condemning the Smithsonian's original script, the atomic bombs have been enshrined in the collective memory of the United States as having been "momentous in helping to bring World War II to a merciful end." To most Americans, the bombs marked THE END in capital letters, so to speak.

The Bombs as the Beginning of Suffering

However, the bombings also were a beginning in two ways. One involved those who survived. For these survivors—we call them *hibakusha*, which literally means those who were exposed to the bombs—suffering began on 6 August or 9 August 1945. Life has remained a living hell to this day, filled with constant fear of radiation disease and death, and even anxiety over possibly passing genetic problems on to one's offspring. Today there are approximately 350,000 survivors of the two atomic bombs. The great majority naturally live in Japan, but there are significant numbers of survivors in both North and South Korea. Many of the South Korean *hibakusha* have been identified and now are asking the Japanese government for compensation because they were victims of Japanese colonialism in that most of them were in the two cities as forced laborers when the bombs were dropped.

Also, little known to most Americans, there are somewhat less than 1,000 U.S. *hibakusha* living in Hawaii and the continental

United States. Most of them are nisei—second-generation Japanese Americans—who for one reason or another were trapped in Japan when the war broke out. Since the mid-1970s they have been asking the U.S. government to provide medical care, but to no avail. For all these surviving victims, the war never really has ended. In fact, they themselves are a living history testifying to the enduring horror of the atomic bombings.

In a second sense, August 1945 also was a beginning rather than an end: the beginning of a new era called the nuclear age.

It all started with Hiroshima and Nagasaki—the spiraling nuclear arms race, accompanied by thousands of nuclear tests causing deadly contamination; nuclear proliferation to many countries; and the so-called peaceful use of nuclear energy, which has brought out the immense inherent risks of nuclear power plants. It is hardly an exaggeration to say that Hiroshima could be the beginning of the end of human beings.

Power Versus Misery

In the early 1960s Oe Kenzaburo, the [1994] Nobel Prize laureate for literature, authored a small book of reportage entitled *Hiroshima Noto* (Hiroshima notes). This was a pioneering work on the human suffering caused by the bombing. In that book, Oe introduced a journalist named Kanai Toshiro, an editorial writer for the *"Chugoku Shimbun,"* a Hiroshima newspaper. Although not a survivor himself, Kanai emerged as a strong advocate urging a reluctant Japanese government to compile a white paper [an official report] on the atomic bombings. The almost pathetic question he raised was this: "Is the atomic bomb better known for its power or for the human misery it caused?" To this, Kanai himself gave the obvious answer. As Oe put it, "Hiroshima and Nagasaki are clearly known throughout the world because the power of the atomic bomb was demonstrated there, not because of the suffering of the A-bomb victims."

That the atomic bomb was the utmost demonstration of U.S. military power and technology was all too clear from President [Harry S.] Truman's statements right after the bombing of Hiroshima. The [1994] aborted plan to use the nuclear mushroom cloud as a design for a postage stamp commemorating the end of the war against Japan demonstrates how this image lingers in the American mind as a symbol of invincible U.S. power.

As the Cold War intensified, the United States devoted itself to enhancing this awesome power, the Soviets followed suit, then Great Britain, China, and France. All these nuclear powers succeeded in creating nuclear arsenals that vastly transcended the destructive power of the Hiroshima bomb. As Kanai lamented, "the nations of the World tend to ignore or forget the great human misery caused by the 'smaller' bomb."

When the Smithsonian's board of trustees decided to cancel its planned exhibition, the victims of Hiroshima and Nagasaki were, in a way, killed again. Because the original plan emphasized the human aspects of the bombing, it was strongly opposed by the American Legion, the Air Force Association, conservative Congressmen, and a large part of the U.S. media. Those in positions of power won out again. And the victims whose misery was not allowed expression were silenced again.

We should listen to the voices of the survivors. Their concern is not primarily with the past, but rather with the past as prologue to the future. Again I quote Kanai Toshiro from Oe Kenzaburo's book: "The fervent desire of the A-bomb victims now, on behalf of all the dead and all survivors, is to ensure that people of the world fully understand the nature and extent of the human mis-

The atomic bomb dropped on Hiroshima killed more than eighty thousand people and left the city in ruins.

ery of an atomic bombing, not just the destructive capacity."

Oe calls these survivors "moralists," by which he means that "they possess unique power of observation and expression concerning what it means to be human." He further says, "the reason they became moralists is that they experienced the cruelest days in human history," and have endured for many years since then. And, again in Oe's words, these survivors have never lost "the vision of a nation that will do its best to materialize a world without any nuclear weapons."

Coming to Terms with the Past

It is understandable that the United States war veterans want to celebrate the glory of their war. Although I was on the wrong side, I envy those who fought "the good war," and I pay full respect to those who gave their last measure for their beloved country. They certainly made history. However, those who make history and those who write it are, or should be, two different kinds of people. Of course, participants can leave memoirs that enrich our understanding of the past. No one, however, participant or not, has any right to dictate how history should be written.

The historian's task is to defrost the past from myth and cook it, so to speak, with newly found evidence and reinterpretations that only historical hindsight can provide. With the distance of half a century, one should be able to see not only the complex and terrible events leading to the mission of the *Enola Gay*, but also the realities of the victims, of Hiroshima and Nagasaki whose living memory can be provided by survivors. The former demands calmness and the latter requires courage—both of which are necessary if we are to attain a level of historical perspective that does justice to all sides.

There are many pitfalls in writing an acceptable public history. One is to make a deal, in which each side cancels out impleas and parts of its own history. Cases in point are Pearl Harbor and Hiroshima/Nagasaki. Here allow me to indulge in a small personal account. In the fall of a 1970 I was in New York City helping to promote an exhibition of murals painted by the artists Maruki Iri and Maruki Toshi depicting the human sufferings of the atomic bombings. On that occasion I paid a courtesy call on a distinguished U.S. professor of Japanese politics and history. When I told him why I was in New York, he became upset and scolded me. "Are you still having such a hangover about Hiroshima? It was a war, and in war death is inevitable. You forget about Hiroshima, then I'll forget about Pearl Harbor."

To this I responded, "No sir. I will not. I admit that Pearl Harbor was a treacherous attack, and I apologize for that. But Hiroshima was the first shot of a nuclear war, quite possibly the beginning of the end of human beings. So we should not forget Hiroshima lest we be doomed." The professor was not convinced, but I still believe that to try to cancel out Hiroshima with Pearl Harbor, or vice versa, is bad history and bad politics. We must remember both events—and all the horrors in between them—lest we repeat the same or more formidable mistakes.

Japan as Victim and Aggressor

This most certainly applies to how the Japanese themselves should present Hiroshima and Nagasaki as public history. The strong sense of being victimized has been widely shared not only by citizens of the two cities but by the Japanese public in general. Many Japanese regard Hiroshima/Nagasaki as another Holocaust: civilian victims died horribly, and survivors are still haunted by their encounter with hell on earth. This memory is so strong that many Japanese tend to regard themselves as innocent victims. Of course the historical fact is that Japan was an aggressor nation and perpetuated unspeakable atrocities. As a partner of Nazi Germany, the perpetrator of the Holocaust, Japan invaded first China and then Southeast Asia, causing immense misery to millions of innocent peoples. And Hiroshima itself was a major military city, home to the large port of Ujina through which millions of soldiers were sent to the battle fronts. Hiroshima also had many factories devoted to war production. The city of Nagasaki was not very different.

The fact that the people of Hiroshima and Nagasaki suffered the bombing, and that survivors are still suffering from aftereffects, does not absolve them from being aggressors. Actually, the atomic bombing was the end result of that war of aggression. When you go to Hiroshima and look into the Peace Memorial Museum there, however, you scarcely see this part of history. (Recent changes in the official Hiroshima exhibition reportedly have improved this situation somewhat, but visitors from Asia unanimously say they have not gone far enough).

If the U.S. critics of the Smithsonian's proposed exhibition are to blame for exercising political pressure to prevent anything but a celebratory presentation of the atomic bombs, those who are behind the Hiroshima Peace Memorial Museum also must be criticized for failing to honestly present the aggressive nature of Japan's war. History must be presented in its totality—its dark as well as triumphant sides. Any decent presentation of the past will provoke controversy, and only through open and honest discussion can we attain higher understanding of the record of human conduct we call history.

Those who use history for political purposes eventually are punished by Clio, the muse of history. Like ostriches in the desert, by burying their heads in the sands of the past they are bound to fail to see the present, let alone the future. The role of public history, I believe, is to help people look back freely on the past in order to understand the murky present—and hopefully, with that light from the past, to illuminate the path toward a yet unknown future.

Defending the Use of the Atomic Bomb

by Winston S. Churchill

Winston S. Churchill (1874–1965) is remembered as one of England's most honorable and dedicated prime ministers. He distinguished himself in the military before serving in England's Parliament for more than sixty years, twice as prime minister. Although a speech defect and poor impromptu debating skills hampered Churchill's first speeches in Parliament, he overcame these difficulties to become one of the world's most respected public speakers. As England's prime minister during most of World War II, he demonstrated his abilities as a leader, strategist, diplomat, and orator. He was tireless in his role as a defender of democracy and a warrior against tyranny and injustice. During the 1930s, Churchill (not yet prime minister) was suspicious of Nazi motives and repeatedly warned political leaders about their rise to power. Later, after World War II ended, he warned about the rise of Soviet power, a warning that proved wise during the Cold War.

Queen Elizabeth II honored Churchill's devotion to his country by knighting him in 1953. Ten years later, the U.S. Congress and President John F. Kennedy recognized him by making him an honorary American citizen. Churchill's last years were spent writing, painting, breeding horses, and overseeing a farm. He died on January 24, 1965, at the age of ninety.

During World War II, Churchill was a powerful Allied leader. He was among American president Harry S. Truman's staunch supporters and held nothing back in defending Truman's tortuous decision to drop the atomic bomb on Japan. Addressing Parliament at the end of World War II, Churchill was unapologetic about the necessity of bombing Hiroshima and Nagasaki. He defended the unprecedented strike and offered reassurance to his fellow political leaders.

O
n 17th July there came to us at Potsdam the eagerly-awaited news of the trial of the atomic bomb in the [New] Mexican desert. Success beyond all dreams crowned this sombre, magnificent venture of our American Allies. The detailed reports of the [New] Mexican desert experiment, which were brought to us a few days later by air, could leave no doubt in the minds of the very few who were informed, that we were in the presence of a new factor in human affairs, and possessed of powers which were irresistible. Great Britain had a right to be consulted in accordance with Anglo-American agreements. The decision to use the atomic bomb was taken by President Truman and myself at Potsdam, and we approved the military plans to unchain the dread, pent-up forces.

From that moment our outlook on the future was transformed. . . .

A Final Ultimatum to Japan

Before using it, it was necessary first of all to send a message in the form of an ultimatum to the Japanese which would apprise them of what unconditional surrender meant. . . . The assurances given to Japan about her future after her unconditional surrender had been made were generous in the extreme. When we remember the cruel and treacherous nature of the utterly unprovoked attack made by the Japanese war lords upon the United States and Great Britain, these assurances must be considered magnanimous in a high degree. . . .

Thus everything in human power, prior to using the atomic bomb, was done to spare the civil population of Japan. There are voices which assert that the bomb should never have been used at all. I cannot associate myself with such ideas. Six years of total war have convinced most people that had the Germans or Japanese discovered this new weapon, they would have used it upon us to our complete destruction with the utmost alacrity. I am surprised that very worthy people, but people who in most cases had no intention of proceeding to the Japanese front themselves, should adopt the position that rather than throw this bomb, we should have sacrificed a million American, and a quarter of a million British lives in the desperate battles and massacres of an invasion of Japan. Future generations will judge these dire decisions, and I believe that if they find themselves dwelling in a happier world from which war has been banished, and where freedom reigns, they will not condemn those who struggled for their benefit amid the horrors and miseries of this gruesome and ferocious epoch.

The bomb brought peace, but men alone can keep that peace, and henceforward they will keep it under penalties which threaten the survival, not only of civilization but of humanity itself. I may say that I am in entire agreement with the President that the secrets of the atomic bomb should so far as possible not be imparted at the present time to any other country in the world. This is in no design or wish for arbitrary power, but for the common safety of the world. Nothing can stop the progress of research and experiment in every country, but although research will no doubt proceed in many places, the construction of the immense plants necessary to transform theory into action cannot be improvised in any country.

For this and many other reasons the United States stand at this moment at the summit of the world. I rejoice that this should be so. Let them act up to the level of their power and their responsibility, not for themselves but for others, for all men in all lands, and then a brighter day may dawn upon human history. . . .

At Last, the War Is Over

It is a time not only of rejoicing but even more of resolve. When we look back on all the perils through which we have passed and at the mighty foes we have laid low and all the dark and deadly designs we have frustrated, why should we fear for our future? We have come safely through the worst.

Home is the sailor, home from sea. And the hunter home from the hill.

The Nuremberg Trials Ushered in a New International Legal Code

by William J. Bosch

The Nuremberg trials offered a much-needed sense of justice in the wake of the horrors committed by the Nazi regime during World War II. The trials also brought to light the need to establish and enforce strong international dictates on wartime behavior. The decisive actions taken by the Nuremberg tribunal empowered future efforts, such as the Tokyo trials, where a similar tribunal tried Japanese leaders from May 1946 to November 1948.

Prior to the Nuremberg trials, efforts had been made to establish international rules of wartime conduct. These precursors to Nuremberg were important in providing common ground among the four Allied nations—the United States, Great Britain, Russia, and France—as they set about the difficult task of agreeing on the authority and objectives of the Nuremberg tribunal. Foremost among Nuremberg's precursors was the Geneva Convention, established in 1929 (and expanded after Nuremberg in 1949). The Geneva Convention is the international mandate on treatment of prisoners of war.

The following excerpt is taken from *Judgment on Nuremberg: American Attitudes Toward the Major German War-Crime Trials* by William J. Bosch. Bosch is a Jesuit priest who has taught history

William J. Bosch, *Judgment on Nuremberg: American Attitudes Toward the Major German War-Crime Trials*. Chapel Hill: The University of North Carolina Press, 1970. Copyright
© 1970 by The University of North Carolina Press. Reproduced by permission.

and modern civilization at the University of North Carolina in Chapel Hill and LeMoyne College in Syracuse, New York.

B old headlines August 9, 1945 announced: "Soviet Declares War on Japan; Attacks Manchuria, Tokyo Says: Atom Bomb Loosed on Nagasaki." At the bottom of this first page was the headline: "4 Powers Call Aggression Crime In Accord Covering War Trials."

Ironically, man's vast potential for destruction overshadowed the efforts which he was making at that moment to bridle the evils of aggression. The Allied nations' signing of the London Charter, which provided the law and procedures for the Nuremberg war-crime trials, hardly competed with the news of weapons that would be able to destroy the human race.

Although the search for safeguards for the rights of men and nations began centuries ago, never before has success in this seeking been so imperative. Modern communications and transportation have brought men closer in their destinies. Apart from the potency of new weapons, this closeness would be less disturbing if the future were not so imperiled by the emergence of modern totalitarianism with its tendency to violate the rights of its citizens and of neighboring states.

Opponents of totalitarianism have tried desperately to devise defenses against aggression and atrocities. Leaders have sought safeguards in several ways: politically, through collective security; militarily, through intimidating destructive might; and economically, through sanctions or elimination of frustrating poverty.

Another major effort to stop unjust wars and violations of human rights has been the development of an international legal code. Many hope that as individual states have curbed internal unrest and made men secure in their rights to life, liberty, and property, so the law of the nations might check international outlawry. "Peace through law" has been a vision which has especially captivated America. Proud of the freedom and security provided by its legal tradition, the United States frequently has attempted through law to solve the nation's and the world's problems.

A Tribunal to Solidify International Law

Perhaps the most striking illustration of this policy was the International Military Tribunal which tried Nazi Germany's leaders after the Second World War. The court which judged Hitler's warlords was significant not only because of the defendants' rank and the depravity and magnitude of their crimes, but also because the Allies sought to create a new international law through the Tribunal's decisions. Aggressive war was declared the "supreme crime"; national leaders who plotted unjust belligerency were held personally accountable; pleas of "head of state" and "order of superior" no longer bestowed legal immunity; and those who abetted aggressive war by their diplomatic, financial or industrial support were liable for the injustices perpetrated by their nation. In addition, an indictment for crimes against humanity was formulated.

The Nuremberg trials were not an impulsive decision by the Allied governments. They were the culmination of twenty-five years of legal development and psychological preparation. Twentieth-century men started on the road to Nuremberg immediately after World War I. . . .

During the [Second World] war, Allied leaders articulated the view that it was no longer tolerable for national leaders to treat their citizens' lives and fortunes as expendable pawns in an international chess game. Repeatedly President Franklin Roosevelt, Prime Minister Winston Churchill, and Marshal Joseph Stalin threatened Nazis with the dire fate awaiting perpetrators of atrocities. Their intent to punish was formally proclaimed in the November 1, 1943 protocol of the Moscow Conference.

The threatened sanctions could fall upon Nazi leaders in a variety of ways. There existed such alternatives as drumhead court-martial [which is a summary court-martial reviewing wartime offenses] summary execution by executive decree [authorized on-the-spot execution], and trial by enemy national courts, by neutral tribunals, or by an international criminal court.

American leaders considered harsh military judgment or executive executions as probably unjust and revolting to the American conscience. Among these leaders were Henry L. Stimson, secretary of war and Robert H. Jackson, an associate justice of the Supreme Court. Such violent solutions, while satisfying a desire for vengeance, would not reassert the rule of law in a world brutalized by the Third Reich's debasing legal order. Nor would such actions preserve the record of Nazi aggression and atrocities. Moreover, trial proponents argued, summary execution would create Nazi martyrs and an opportunity for revisionists and isolationists to claim once more that charges against the German enemy were fabrications.

The alternative of using German courts had little support. Men remembered Leipzig and wished no recurrence of the legal scandal perpetrated there.

The employment of neutral courts was exceedingly attractive and seemed to be a just and equitable method of punishment. Those urging international tribunals, however, held that this appeal was deceptive. They contended that after World War II no true neutral nation existed, for no state had refrained from hostilities because it was uninterested or impartial toward the outcome. Indeed a nation's desire for neutrality frequently had little relation to its actual status. Moreover, in states termed neutral the legal and political leaders had in fact chosen sides, or at least their self-interest was connected with one or the other of the belligerents. Finally, it would be hard to find a man who was neutral to [the Nazi death camps of] Dachau and Buchenwald, and, if such a man were found, would one wish him to sit in judgment?

The Formation of the Tribunal and Its Objectives

By January of 1945 the United States government decided to conduct international trials. The three other major Allied powers accepted the American program at the San Francisco United Nations Conference.

Meetings in London during the summer of 1945, attended by representatives of the United States, Great Britain, the Soviet Union, and the provisional government of France, marked the inception of the Allies' postwar punishment program. Associate Justice Robert Jackson, appointed by President Harry Truman as head of the United States delegation and future chief counsel for the American prosecution, was both guiding spirit and practical planner for the conference.

Almost insurmountable problems faced Jackson. He had to write the law for the court, reconcile four legal traditions, blend four courtroom procedures, and overcome the obstacle of five different languages.

Solutions to these problems and many others were embodied in the London Agreement and Charter signed August 8, 1945. The agreement expressed the will of the Allies to create an International Military Tribunal to judge major Nazi criminals. The agreement further declared that the charter, which determined the court's constitution and jurisdiction, was the Tribunal's supreme law and that all of its provisions would be unchallengeable by prosecution or defense. The Big Four finally stated that other governments could adhere to the agreement, and nineteen members of the United Nations accepted this invitation.

The charter itself contained the law and procedure of Nuremberg. It determined the judicial character of the International Military Tribunal and the composition of the bench. The document stated that the defendants would be those whose crimes fell within three basic categories: crimes against peace, which consisted of conspiring, initiating, or waging a war of aggression; war crimes, which included all the traditional violations of the laws or customs of war; and crimes against humanity, which covered the atrocities of deportation, enslavement, and genocide.

The charter further determined that the governmental position of defendants as heads of state could not confer immunity from punishment nor could such a defense be urged even to mitigate penalties. The defendant's plea that he was following the orders of superiors did not free him from responsibility, though it could be a factor in lessening punishment.

Finally, the charter dealt with the problem of organizational guilt. The document declared that the Tribunal might proscribe a group or organization as being essentially criminal in its orientation. If this were decided, prosecuting nations had the right to bring any individual to trial for membership in such a body.

Nuremberg Is Chosen as the Location

Once the Allies had created the law and the judicial forms needed for trying the Nazis, a location for the trials had to be determined. The Russian prosecutor opted for Berlin on the ground that it was the former capital of the fallen foe. This suggestion was rejected for the simple reason that Allied destruction of Berlin had been so complete that no building of the size necessary for a large-scale trial remained intact.

The pragmatic consideration of physical facilities led the Allies to choose Nuremberg for the International Military Tribunal. Although bombs had destroyed large areas, the medieval Palace of Justice and the large prison still stood amid the rubble. These buildings provided accommodations for detention of prisoners and conduction of trials.

If practical aspects determined the choice of Nuremberg, no one was oblivious to the symbolism of the selection. During former September days and nights Nuremberg was the Bavarian city that had witnessed the spectacle of the Nazi party rallies. Its streets and walls had echoed with four hundred thousand strident voices of Hitler's triumphant legions shouting "*Sieg Heil!*"; its stone stadium had reverberated with the drums and bugles heralding a New Order which was to last a thousand years. Moreover, the infamous decrees which deprived German-Jews of their legal rights and left them defenseless against the atrocities to come were entitled the Nuremberg laws.

The Breadth of the Trials and Their Judgments

By common agreement twenty-four Nazis were selected for trial before the International Military Tribunal. Of these, Robert Ley, leader of the German Labor Front, committed suicide; Gustav Krupp, head of the Krupp munitions works, was declared too senile to stand trial; and Martin Bormann, head of the Party Chancery, was tried "in absentia." Twenty-one defendants, therefore, were arraigned at Nuremberg.

The trials started November 20, 1945 and ended August 31, 1946. The court conducted 403 open sessions. During the trials, 113 witnesses were called, 33 for the prosecution and 80 for the defense. One hundred thousand documents were accepted by the court. Five million words were recorded in evidence.

Final judgment was delivered September 30 and October 1, 1946. Ten of the defendants were sentenced to death by hanging. [Hermann] Goering, one of the condemned, cheated the hangman by suicide. Three defendants received life imprisonment; four were given prison sentences ranging from ten to twenty years; three were acquitted.

Five organizations were declared criminal: the leadership corps of the Nazi party; the SS (Schutzstaffel), an elite corps under [Heinrich] Himmler; the SD (Sicherheitsdienst), a security Service; the SA (Sturmabteilung), a paramilitary organization; and the Gestapo, the secret state police. The judges demanded, however, that personal responsibility for crimes be proved in any subsequent trial of members of these groups. The court decided that the Reich Cabinet and the General Staff and High Command of the German Armed Forces lacked the cohesiveness required of an "organization" under the London Charter and therefore could not be condemned as criminal groups.

Nuremberg's Legacy

Thus ended the first great international criminal trial. But in many ways Nuremberg was just beginning. The length and the expense of the proceedings made other formal international tribunals unacceptable to the Allies, but courts of each of the four Allied powers and of the Germans themselves carried on the work of trying alleged Nazi offenders. When the denazification process was completed by 1950, these latter courts had tried over 3,500,000 Germans, using elements of Nuremberg's procedure and law. Some of the Tribunal's principles were also embodied in such documents as the peace treaties with individual defeated nations, the army manuals of discipline for numerous countries, and other new national and international enactments. Nuremberg established for better or worse new developments in international law which had many future ramifications.

The Tribunal's most significant innovation was its legal definition of aggression as the "supreme crime." The novelty of this Nuremberg charge was that before the Tribunal's verdicts international law considered all wars ethically neutral and politically justifiable if a state deemed such belligerent action essential to its national interests. The court, going beyond even the dreams of those who wished to revive the concept that wars were either just or unjust, declared that aggression not only violated moral norms but also transgressed international law. Indeed, the judges asserted that aggression was the greatest of legal crimes for which death was the only fit penalty. Those who caused the murder of millions must pay with their lives.

A second principle enunciated was that government leaders were personally responsible for their policies. Previously, being a head of state created immunity from criminal liability. Decisions of political authorities were considered referrable to an abstract entity which was independent, sovereign, and supreme in its own affairs.

Nuremberg declared all this changed. Government leaders no longer could hide behind the shield of "head of state" or "order of superior." The court and the charter maintained that international law can touch individuals within each nation in a fashion analogous to the operation of United States federal law within the particular states. As the Nuremberg judges asserted: ". . . the very essence of the Charter is that individuals have international duties which transcend the national obligations of obedience imposed by the individual state." Most of the other Nuremberg principles were corollaries of these two major innovations—the criminality of aggression and personal responsibility.

Another decision important for the future was that all who aided criminal policies would stand trial as well as those who formulated the ultimate decisions for aggression and atrocities. Consequently, diplomats and financiers, industrialists and soldiers, all who make modern war possible could be called to account by international tribunals.

The judges, perceiving that the modern totalitarian state had the power to strangle its neighbors and to purge whole groups and organizations, nations, and races, enforced new laws condemning crimes against humanity. Previously, the rules and customs of war were adequate to sanction outrages because war crimes such as murder, looting, or rape were usually restricted to deeds of individual soldiers. At most, some commander might issue an order which resulted in a barbarity, but Nazism presented a different problem. Here was not an isolated outrage but a number of deliberate, extended policies officially adopted by a recognized government and executed by large organizations in a systematic fashion. The Nuremberg court decreed that not only the men who shot hostages and civilians, not only the men who turned on the gas in the chamber, but the political leaders who signed the orders and the propaganda chiefs who created the hysteria favorable to such genocide must pay for crimes against humanity.

Finally the Tribunal established a precedent demanding that any person charged with criminal action in international law has a right to a fair trial. Anyone accused can demand that all the safeguards of due process be afforded him.

Excerpts from the Nuremberg Trial Transcripts

Lasting from November 20, 1945, to August 31, 1946, the Nuremberg trials were a tribunal that tried key Nazi leaders on four counts: participation in a common plan or conspiracy to commit crimes against peace, war crimes, and crimes against humanity; commission of crimes against peace; commission of war crimes; and commission of crimes against humanity. The unprecedented trials were held both because of the systematic murder of millions of Jews, Gypsies, Poles, and members of other groups, and because nations that had suffered under the Nazis wanted to punish the ringleaders. The tribunal included two judges from each of the four Allied nations (the United States, Great Britain, France, and the Soviet Union); one judge from each country served as a member, and the second served as an alternate. The tribunal's charter stated that the accused could be held responsible for his actions, even if he was carrying out the orders of a superior officer.

Twenty-four people were to stand trial, but only twenty-two were ultimately tried because one committed suicide and another was determined physically and mentally unfit. Adolf Hitler, Joseph Paul Goebbels (minister of propaganda), and Heinrich Himmler (chief of the Gestapo) had all committed suicide and thus could not be made answerable for their critical roles in the Third Reich.

The trials were completed after nine months, and the tribunal handed down its decisions. The tribunal acquitted three men and sentenced seven to prison terms of varying lengths, including life. The other defendants were sentenced to death by hanging, which was carried out on the night of October 15. One prisoner escaped hanging by swallowing a vial of poison, an incident that intrigued

Proceedings of the International Military Tribunal in Session at Nuremberg, Germany, November 30, 1945.

people all over the world. How and where he got the poison remains
a mystery.

The following trial excerpt is the interrogation of Major General
Erwin Lahousen, who was a member of the Austrian Intelligence
Service and then of German Armed Forces intelligence during the
war. Lahousen is questioned about the actions of those on trial as a
witness for the prosecution. He was privy to secret meetings and orders during the war, but he was not on trial for committing any war
crimes.

The President: I call on the prosecutor for the United States.
    Mr. Justice [Robert] Jackson: Colonel Amen will repre-
    sent the United States this morning.
    Colonel, John H. Amen: May it please the Tribunal, I propose
to call as the first witness for the prosecution, Major General Erwin Lahousen. . . .
    Q. Now, will you state to the Tribunal what your principal ac-
tivities were after being assigned to the Intelligence Division?
What information were you interested in and seeking to obtain?
    A. If I understand your question correctly, I was a member of
the Austrian Intelligence Service, that is to say, in the Austrian
Intelligence Service and not in the German so-called "Abwehr."
    Q. After the Anschluss, what position did you assume?
    A. After the Anschluss I was automatically taken into the High
Command of the German Armed Forces, and did the same job
there. My chief there was Admiral [Wilhelm] Canaris.
    Q. And what was the position of Admiral Canaris?
    A. Canaris was, at that time, Chief of the Bureau of the
"Ausland-Abwehr," that is to say, of the Intelligence. . . .

Lahousen's Meetings with Hitler and Others

Q. Now, do you recall attending conferences with Canaris at the
Führer headquarters just prior to the fall of Warsaw?
    A. I and Canaris took part in a conference which did not take
place in the Führer's headquarters, but in the so-called Führer's
train, shortly before the fall of Warsaw.
    Q. And having refreshed your recollection from reference to
the entries in Canaris' diary, can you tell the Tribunal the date of
those conferences?

A. According to the notes and documents at my disposal, it was on 12th September, 1939.

Q. Did each of these conferences take place on the same day?

A. The conferences in the Führer's train took place on 12th September, 1939.

Q. And was there more than one conference on that day? Were they split into several conferences?

A. I cannot call them sessions; they were discussions, conversations, of shorter or longer duration, but not actually conferences.

Q. And who was present on this occasion?

A. Present, independent of time and location, were the following: Foreign Minister [Joachim] von Ribbentrop; [Wilhelm] Keitel, the Chief of the O.K.W. [armed forces], the president of the "Wehrmacht-Führungstab" at that time, [Alfred] Jodl; Canaris; and myself. . . .

Lahousen Recalls Plans for Poland

Q. Now, to the best of your knowledge and recollection, will you please explain, in as much detail as possible, to the Tribunal, exactly what was said and what took place at this conference in the Führer's train?

A. First of all, Canaris had a short talk with Ribbentrop, in which von Ribbentrop explained political aims in general, with regard to the Polish regions, and in particular with regard to the Ukranian question. Later the Chief of the O.K.W. took up the Ukrainian question in subsequent discussions which took place in his private working carriage. These are recorded in the notes which I took down immediately, on Canaris' commission. While we were still in the train of the Chief of the O.K.W., Canaris expressed serious scruples regarding the bombardment of Warsaw, stressing the devastating repercussions on foreign policy of such a bombardment. The Chief of the O.K.W., at that time, Keitel, answered that these measures had been laid down directly by the Führer and [Hermann] Göring, and that he, Keitel, had had no influence on these decisions. He spoke these words—I can repeat them only after having read my notes; the Führer and Göring telephoned frequently back and forth; sometimes I heard something of what was said, but not always.

Secondly, Canaris gave an earnest warning against the measures which he knew about, i.e., the projected shooting and extermination which were to be directed particularly against the

Polish intelligentsia, the nobility, the clergy, as well as all elements that could be regarded as embodying the national resistance movement. Canaris said at that time—I am quoting more
or less verbatim—"the world will at some time make the armed
forces under whose eyes these events occurred also responsible
for these events."

The then Chief of the O.K.W. replied—and what I am now going to say is based on my notes, which I looked through a few
days ago—that these things had been determined by the Führer,
and that the Führer, the Commander in Chief of the Army, had
made it known that, should the armed forced refuse to have any
part in these things or should they not agree with them, they
would have to accept the fact that the S.S., the S.I.P.O. and such
organisations would be simultaneously employed to carry out
these very measures. Thus, at the side of each military commander, a corresponding civilian official would be appointed. This,
in outline, was the subject of the discussion dealing with extermination measures and the policy of shooting.

Poles Are Singled Out for Execution

Q. Was anything said about a so-called political house-cleaning?

A. Yes, the then Chief of the O.K.W. used an expression in this
connection which was certainly derived from Hitler, and which
characterised these measures as "political house-cleaning." This
expression remains very clearly in my recollection without the
aid of my notes.

Q. In order that the record may be perfectly clear, exactly what
measure did Keitel say had already been agreed upon?

A. According to the then Chief of the O.K.W., the bombardment of Warsaw and the shooting of those categories of people
whom I characterised before, had been agreed upon already.

Q. And what were they?

A. Foremost of all, the Polish intelligentsia, the nobility, the
clergy, and, of course, the Jews.

Q. What, if anything, was said about possible co-operation
with a Ukrainian group?

A. Canaris was ordered by the then Chief of the O.K.W., who
stated that he was transmitting a directive which he had apparently received from Ribbentrop in connection with the political
plans of the Foreign Minister, to instigate a resistance movement
in the Galician part of the Ukraine, which should have as its goal

the extermination of Jews and Poles.

Q. At what point did Hitler and Jodl enter this meeting?

A. Hitler and Jodl entered either after what I have just described took place, or towards the conclusion of this discussion, and Canaris had already begun his report on the situation in the West: that is to say, on the news that had come in in the meantime, regarding the attitude of the French army at the West Wall.

Q. And what further discussions took place then?

A. After this discussion in the private working carriage of the Chief of the O.K.W., Canaris left the coach and had a short talk with Ribbentrop, who, returning to the theme of the Ukraine, told him once more that the uprising or the resistance movement should be so arranged that all farms and dwellings of the Poles should go up in flames, and all Jews be killed.

Q. Who said that?

A. The Foreign Minister at that time, Ribbentrop, said this to Canaris. I was standing next to him.

Q. Is there any slightest doubt in your mind about that?

A. No. I have not the slightest doubt about that. I remember with particular clarity the somewhat new formulation that "all farms and dwellings should go up in flames" because previously only terms like "liquidation" and "killing" had been used.

Q. Was there any note in Canaris' diary which helped to refresh your recollection on that point also?

A. No.

Q. What, if anything, was said on the subject of France?

A. On the subject of France a discussion took place in the carriage of the Chief of the O.K.W. Canaris explained the situation in the West according to reports he had received from the "Abwehr" intelligence service. Canaris described the situation by saying that in his opinion a great attack was being prepared by the French in the sector of Saarbrücken. Hitler, who had entered the room in the meantime, intervened, took charge of the discussion and rejected in a lively manner the opinion which Canaris had just expressed, putting forward arguments which, looking back now, I must recognise as factually correct.

Q. Do you recall whether, in the course of this conference, Ribbentrop said anything about the Jews?

A. During the conversation, which was taking place in the private conference coach of the Chief of the O.K.W., Ribbentrop was not present.

Q. Do you recall whether at any time in the course of the conferences Ribbentrop said anything about the Jews?

A. In this discussion, I repeat—the one that took place in the coach—no.

Q. For purposes of keeping the record straight, whenever you have referred to the Chief of the O.K.W., you were referring to Keitel?

A. Yes.

Concentration Camp Inmates and the Polish Resistance

Q. Was the Wehrmacht ever asked to furnish any resistance for the Polish campaign?

A. Yes.

Q. Did that undertaking have any special name?

A. As it is recorded in the diary of my section, the name of this undertaking that took place just before the Polish campaign, was given the name "Himmler."

Q. Will you explain to the Tribunal the nature of the assistance required?

A. The matter in which I am now giving testimony is one of the most mysterious actions which took place in the atmosphere of the Abwehr office. Sometime, I believe it was the middle of August—the precise date can be found in the corresponding entry of the diary—Abwehr Section I, as well as my section, Abwehr Section II, were charged with the job of providing or keeping in readiness Polish uniforms and equipment, as well as identification cards, and so on, for the undertaking "Himmler." This request, according to an entry in my diary made by my aide-de-camp, was received by Canaris from the Wehrmacht Führungstab or from the "Landesverteidigung"—National Defence.

Q. Do you know whence this request originated?

A. Whence the request originated I cannot say. I can only repeat how it reached us in the form of an order. It was, to be sure, an order on which was the chiefs of sections concerned, already had some misgivings without knowing what, in the last analysis, it was about. The name Himmler, however, was eloquent enough. In the pertinent entries of the diary, expression is given to the fact that I asked the question why Mr. Himmler was to receive uniforms from us.

Q. To whom was the Polish material to be furnished by the Abwehr?

A. These articles of equipment had to be kept in readiness, and one day some man from the S.S. or the S.D.—the name is given in the official war-diary of the department—fetched them.

Q. At what time was the Abwehr informed as to how this Polish material was to be used?

A. The real purpose, which we do not know in its details even today, was concealed from us, we did not learn it, though at the time we had a very understandable suspicion that something crooked was afoot, particularly because of the name of the undertaking.

Q. Did you subsequently find out from Canaris what in fact had happened?

A. The actual course of events was the following: When the first war-bulletin appeared, which spoke of the attack of Polish units on German territory, Pieckenbrock, who had the report in his hand, and read it, observed that now we knew what our uniforms had been needed for. The same day or a few days later, I cannot say exactly, Canaris informed us that people from concentration camps disguised in these uniforms had been ordered to make a military attack on the radio station at Gleiwitz. I cannot recall whether any other locality was mentioned. Although we were greatly interested . . . to learn details of this action, that is, where it had occurred and what had happened in detail—as a matter of fact we could well imagine it—we did not know for certain, and I cannot even today say exactly what happened.

Q. Did you ever find out what happened to the men from the concentration camps that wore the Polish uniforms and created the incident?

A. It is strange, this matter held my interest ever since, so much so that even after the capitulation, I spoke about these matters with an S.S. Haupt-Sturnführer who was confined in the same hospital as I was, and I asked him for details on what had taken place. The man—his name was Birckel—told me, "It is peculiar, but even we in our circles only found out about these matters much, much after, and then what we did find out was only by implication. So far as I know," he said, "all members of the S.D. who took part in that action were presumably put out of the way; that is to say, were killed." That is the last I heard of this matter.

The Truman Doctrine Initiates the Cold War

by Lynn Boyd Hinds and Theodore Otto Windt Jr.

The Cold War lasted from the end of World War II (although some historians argue that it had its slow beginnings before the war was over) until about 1990. During this time, tensions between the United States and the Soviet Union deepened as each denounced the other's fundamental social and political systems. When President Harry Truman delivered his doctrine of "containment," he took a bold step on behalf of the United States, declaring that totalitarianism was unacceptable and that the United States would support nations everywhere who opposed it. Truman set forth a new ideological approach to foreign affairs that would apply to other nations in the future.

The ideological aspect of the Truman Doctrine is important. Truman proposed a new way of thinking about global politics that was not based on military strategy, economic stability, or repaying favors. The Truman Doctrine declared that the United States, as a democracy, would work to promote democracy in other parts of the world as a matter of principle. The villains in his scenario were totalitarian regimes such as those instituted by Communists. Because of the philosophical undercurrent of the Cold War, persuasion and rhetoric became prominent. The goal of preventing communism from spreading dominated foreign policy for more than forty years.

Lynn Boyd Hinds and Theodore Otto Windt Jr. are professional journalists and professors. Hinds has enjoyed a career as a producer

Lynn Boyd Hinds and Theodore Otto Windt Jr., *The Cold War as Rhetoric: The Beginnings, 1945–1950*. Westport, CT: Praeger Publishers, 1991. Copyright © 1991 by Lynn Boyd Hinds and Theodore Otto Windt Jr. Reproduced by permission.

and scholar of mass media. Windt is an author and a political commentator and consultant.

I n his address to a joint session of Congress on March 12, 1947 President Truman officially committed the United States to an ideological cold war. *Newsweek* magazine called it "America's Date with Destiny." With unmistakable clarity Truman stated the principle that would guide U.S. global strategy for the next four decades: "I believe it must be the policy of the United States to support free people who are resisting attempted subjugation by armed minorities or by outside pressures." As many recognized at the time, it represented a new foreign policy for the United States. The day after the speech, James Reston of the *New York Times* compared its significance to that of the Monroe Doctrine [which detailed the U.S. policies concerning Europe], and it quickly became known as the "Truman Doctrine."

A Transformation of the Presidency and the Nation

The speech led to a transformation of Harry Truman and a transformation of U.S. foreign policy. Those transformations had been more than a year in the making. From the end of 1945 when concern over Soviet maneuvers turned to alarm, the administration had begun narrowing its perceptions and its options. Now, in March 1947 it was time to announce publicly this policy transformation. Truman's address built on the division [British prime minister Winston] Churchill had drawn at Fulton, placed ideological themes and arguments drawn from Churchill and from the Clifford-Elsey report [a crucial report on Soviet expansionism] in an American policy context, and transformed that policy (that, for all practical purposes, had been in effect for a year) into a doctrine, a doctrine that would form the basis for the anticommunist reality of subsequent decades. Truman described it as "this terrible decision" and Margaret Truman concluded that it was "the real beginning of the cold war." The president's speech defined a new ideological reality that would dominate the American political arena in which foreign policy commitments (and many domestic policies, as well) would be debated and either implemented or rejected.

Truman's historic proclamation, taken with the other rhetorical events of this period, resulted in a transformation of American society. . . .

A New Ideological Perspective

In eighteen minutes President Truman had announced a significant departure in America's traditional foreign policy and had created a new way of seeing its place in the postwar world. He had created a simple good-evil perceptual lens through which the American people could view, understand, interpret, and act upon events that the administration said symbolized confrontations between two mutually exclusive "ways of life." Differences within the so-called free world and within the so-called communist world were minimized or ignored, as the moral and mortal conflict between the two was accentuated. About such language as this, Alexis de Tocqueville [author of *Democracy in America*] had observed: "Democratic writers are perpetually coining abstract words . . . in which they sublimate into further abstraction the abstract terms of the language. Moreover, to render their mode of speech more succinct, they personify the object of these abstract terms and make it act like a real person." The personifications would come later. For the moment, the abstract definition of the enemy and the abstract principle would suffice. As one Briton said: "We went to sleep in one world and woke up . . . in another.". . .

Harry S. Truman

Positive Responses

Probably the most accurate summary of reaction to the speech was that both the press and Congress recognized the speech as a landmark in U.S. history. The *New York Times*'s headline stated: "TRUMAN ACTS TO SAVE NATIONS FROM RED RULE." The first paragraph of its news story succinctly captured the meaning of the speech: "President Truman outlined a new foreign policy for the United States today. In a historic message to Congress, he proposed that this country intervene wherever necessary throughout the world to prevent the subjection of free peo-

ples to Communist-inspired totalitarian regimes at the expense
of their national integrity and importance." James Reston compared Truman's policy to that of the Monroe Doctrine and [Pres-
ident Franklin D.] Roosevelt's announcement of the lend-lease
program. The lead editorial in the *Times* went further: "This was
a speech comparable with President Roosevelt's famous 'quar-
antine'" speech against aggressors, a speech made under analogous circumstances in 1937. The Omaha *World Herald* rightly
called the speech "the most breath-taking statement ever made
in time of peace by any American President or statesman."

The weekly magazines also joined the chorus of praise. *Life* ed-
itorialized that "the immediate task of America is to hold the door
of history open for the kind of world government which lovers of
freedom can approve." *Time, Newsweek,* and the *New Leader* carried a number of stories on the speech that ranged from approving
to enthusiastic. David Lawrence, editor of *U.S. News,* gave the
strongest endorsement: "If American Presidents from 1920 to 1939
had made it plain beforehand that the United States meant to use
her industrial, financial, and military power to checkmate aggression, the Second World War would never have been fought."

Negative Reactions

Domestic criticism of Truman's speech came primarily from iso-
lationist forces on the right and the old FDR forces on the left
(left of Truman, that is). The reasons for their criticism or opposition were just as diverse. On the conservative side, Senator
[Robert] Taft remarked that if the United States assumed a "special position in Greece and Turkey . . . we can hardly . . . object
to Russians continuing their domination in Poland, Yugoslavia,
Rumania, and Bulgaria." Representative Harold Knutson of Min-
nesota objected to the economic commitment: "I guess the do-
gooders won't feel right until they have us all broke." On the liberal side, both *Nation* magazine and *The New Republic* inveighed
against the Truman Doctrine. The former stated: "Blindly, without general public understanding or consent, without even a clear
picture of what lies at the end, the United States takes its first
steps along the road of big-power politics." Henry Wallace was
even more vehement. He wrote that the speech had "scarcely a
paragraph of fact or evidence. All was a mixture of unsupported
assertions, sermonizing and exhortation. It was evident that in
the name of crisis facts had been withheld, time had been denied

and a feeling of panic had been engendered." But the range of criticism as well as the range of political beliefs by the critics, as we shall later discuss, worked against them, especially in contrast to the single consistent message presented by the administration and echoed by the influential press.

The response from the target of the president's warning, the Soviet Union, was curious. On the one hand, *Izvestia* and *Pravda* denounced the speech as "adventurist." *Pravda* charged that Truman's arguments were borrowed from Hitler who "also referred to the Bolshevik danger when he prepared for the seizure of one state or another." It charged that the United States had disregarded its obligations to the United Nations. . . .

The authority with which one speaks directly influences belief. Part of Churchill's authority came from his person. His reputation as spokesman for freedom during World War II required that others weigh his words seriously, even if they rejected them at the time. Harry Truman's authority came from his office. He was president of the United States and he was proposing a sharp departure from traditional U.S. foreign policy. Unlike Churchill, he was in a position to implement that policy. But in this particular case, the speech lent authority to Truman.

Ever since he had been propelled into the presidency, he had been hounded by questions, mainly privately spoken but sometimes voiced in public, about whether he was up to the job. He pondered the same questions himself. With the decisive language and bold policy of this speech, he began to be transformed. Again, this was no overnight or magical transformation. His appointment of General [George C.] Marshall, probably the most esteemed American citizen of the time, as secretary of state in January 1947 enhanced his authority. The other appointments early that year conveyed the image that government by crony was being replaced with government by capability. Secretary Marshall's pointed deference to the president, especially noted in his announcement about the Greek request for aid, added further to recognition of Truman's ultimate responsibility for foreign policy. Yet, these only prepared the way.

Truman had made an historic decision. He had presented it to Congress in an historic speech. He had used little evidence in the speech, and the logic of relating Greece and Turkey to his doctrine was tortured. Yet, the sweep of his proposal and the fears he aroused created a new Harry Truman.

The transformation was immediately noted. Reporters noticed a new briskness to his step. *Newsweek* reported there was no question now whether he would run for election in his own right or not. His personal approval rating that had stood at 32 percent just after the 1946 congressional elections, now had soared to more than 60 percent. Long stories in major magazines now treated him with greater respect. Before the speech at least one writer had called America's upcoming new global strategy, Marshall's policy. Now and forever more, it would be known as the Truman Doctrine. The increasing prestige accorded to the president gave greater authority to his version of reality and the appropriate ways for Americans to deal with it.

Cementing Anticommunist Resolve

On May 22 Truman signed the bill authorizing aid to Greece and Turkey into law. But in the days between February 21 and May 22 much more had happened than a partisan campaign for a political policy. A new reality about the world and America's place in it was announced and began to take hold. The process had begun with Churchill's speech but now it had been Americanized and given an enormous boost by Truman's address. Both Churchill and Truman described a world divided into two irreconcilable ideologies. Whereas Churchill called for an alliance, Truman insisted that only the United States was strong enough to engage in this ideological war. The American way of life was at stake. A world hung in the balance. When Secretary Marshall objected to the extravagance of the speech, the reply was that it was the "only way" the president could get Congress to pass the legislation for aid to Greece. That reply suggests that Truman believed the rhetoric pertained only to this situation and that he had Congress in mind as his principal audience. He may have believed that such universal language and commitments were needed on this specific occasion to pass the enabling legislation and that later he could apply these principles selectively. There is considerable evidence that Truman and his advisers did not believe these principles should be applied to Asia, especially China. But Truman underestimated the powerful impact his speech had and the authority he possessed. The drama of the crisis, the melodramatic presentation of arguments, the sinister enemy who was linked to the just defeated but universally hated Nazis—all came together to produce a growing unity among Americans in opposition to communism. Indeed, the rhetorical threat of a diabolical enemy threatening the world all but obscured the policy of sending aid to Greece and Turkey. Bipartisan support from Democrats and Republicans, reinforced by leading journalistic opinion-makers, made it a common reality beyond partisan differences, beyond the president's power to control or recall it. The extensive publicity generated in the press overwhelmed criticism of this new reality. Those who had the fortitude to question or criticize found themselves consigned to the alien community in which questions about their patriotism were raised. In his brief speech President Harry Truman constructed only the bare bones of an American anticommunist ideology. Others would give flesh and muscle to it.

Communism Must Be Contained

by Harry S. Truman

Born in 1884, Harry S. Truman was reared in and around Independence, Missouri. As a child, he accompanied his father to political meetings, an experience that proved influential. Truman also displayed an early interest in a wide range of topics and became an avid reader. At the age of six, he met a girl named Bess Wallace, whom he married after serving in World War I.

Once he returned from the war and settled into his new life with Bess, Truman became involved in local politics. In 1943 President Franklin D. Roosevelt sought his fourth presidential term and wanted a new running mate to help secure votes. As a senator, Truman had earned a reputation among his peers and his constituents as a man who fought for economic stability and for the rights of ordinary Americans. These qualities made Truman a strong running mate, and he grudgingly accepted Roosevelt's offer. They won. The new vice president knew little of affairs on Capitol Hill, and Roosevelt was too busy with the war to spend much time with him. When Roosevelt died in April 1945, however, Truman found himself president of a nation in the grips of war. Despite his initial discomfort with the heavy mantle of the presidency, Truman grew into his responsibilities. He is famous for the sign on his desk that read, "The buck stops here." His straightforward way of speaking and humble demeanor soon won the approval of the American people. Ironically, Truman is known as the president who gave the orders to drop the atomic bomb on Japan, yet when he first took office, he was not even aware of the bomb's development.

Truman's two terms as president (1945–1953) are remembered for the bombing of Japan, the Truman Doctrine, and the Korean War. In their ways, each of these events represents an aspect of the Cold War. Historians consider the Truman Doctrine, however, to be the midwife of the Cold War because it stated the U.S. intolerance

---

Harry S. Truman, "The Truman Doctrine," address before the U.S. Senate, March 12, 1947.

for communism and set forth a policy of "containment." This meant that the United States would dedicate itself to containing communism and preventing its spread. Truman delivered his containment policy speech in the wake of political unrest in Greece. Greece had been ravaged by war with Turkey, occupation by Italy and Germany during World War II, and a civil war that lasted from 1944 to 1949. The civil war involved the existing government and the Communist-backed National Liberation Front. Luckily for the Greeks, Truman's speech brought about the aid they needed to defeat the Communists.

The effects of the Truman Doctrine were profound and far-reaching. The doctrine shaped foreign policy for decades and placed emphasis on democratic ideals rather than military and economic strategy.

T he gravity of the situation which confronts the world today necessitates my appearance before a joint session of the Congress.

The foreign policy and the national security of this country are involved.

One aspect of the present situation, which I present to you at this time for your consideration and decision, concerns Greece and Turkey.

The United States has received from the Greek Government an urgent appeal for financial and economic assistance. Preliminary reports from the American Economic Mission now in Greece and reports from the American Ambassador in Greece corroborate the statement of the Greek Government that assistance is imperative if Greece is to survive as a free nation. I do not believe that the American people and the Congress wish to turn a deaf ear to the appeal of the Greek Government.

Greece is not a rich country. Lack of sufficient natural resources has always forced the Greek people to work hard to make both ends meet. Since 1940, this industrious, peace loving country has suffered invasion, four years of cruel enemy occupation, and bitter internal strife.

A Threatened Greece

When forces of liberation entered Greece they found that the retreating Germans had destroyed virtually all the railways, roads, port facilities, communications, and merchant marine. More than a thousand villages had been burned. Eighty-five percent of the children were tubercular. Livestock, poultry, and draft animals had almost disappeared. Inflation had wiped out practically all savings.

As a result of these tragic conditions, a militant minority, exploiting human want and misery, was able to create political chaos which, until now, has made economic recovery impossible. Greece is today without funds to finance the importation of those goods which are essential to bare subsistence. Under these circumstances the people of Greece cannot make progress in solving their problems of reconstruction. Greece is in desperate need of financial and economic assistance to enable it to resume purchases of food, clothing, fuel and seeds. These are indispensable for the subsistence of its people and are obtainable only from abroad. Greece must have help to import the goods necessary to restore internal order and security so essential for economic and political recovery.

The Greek Government has also asked for the assistance of experienced American administrators, economists and technicians to insure that the financial and other aid given to Greece shall be used effectively in creating a stable and self-sustaining economy and in improving its public administration.

The very existence of the Greek state is today threatened by the terrorist activities of several thousand armed men, led by Communists, who defy the government's authority at a number of points, particularly along the northern boundaries. A Commission appointed by the United Nations Security Council is at present investigating disturbed conditions in northern Greece and alleged border violations along the frontier between Greece on the one hand and Albania, Bulgaria, and Yugoslavia on the other.

Meanwhile, the Greek Government is unable to cope with the situation. The Greek army is small and poorly equipped. It needs supplies and equipment if it is to restore authority to the government throughout Greek territory. Greece must have assistance if it is to become a self-supporting and self-respecting democracy.

Only the United States Can Help Restore Democracy

The United States must supply this assistance. We have already extended to Greece certain types of relief and economic aid but these are inadequate.

There is no other country to which democratic Greece can turn.

No other nation is willing and able to provide the necessary support for a democratic Greek government.

The British Government, which has been helping Greece, can give no further financial or economic aid after March 31. Great Britain finds itself under the necessity of reducing or liquidating its commitments in several parts of the world, including Greece.

We have considered how the United Nations might assist in this crisis. But the situation is an urgent one requiring immediate action, and the United Nations and its related organizations are not in a position to extend help of the kind that is required.

It is important to note that the Greek Government has asked for our aid in utilizing effectively the financial and other assistance we may give to Greece, and in improving its public administration. It is of the utmost importance that we supervise the use of any funds made available to Greece, in such a manner that each dollar spent will count toward making Greece self-supporting, and will help to build an economy in which a healthy democracy can flourish.

No government is perfect. One of the chief virtues of a democracy, however, is that its defects are always visible and under democratic processes can be pointed out and corrected. The government of Greece is not perfect. Nevertheless it represents 85 percent of the members of the Greek Parliament who were chosen in an election last year. Foreign observers, including 692 Americans, considered this election to be a fair expression of the views of the Greek people.

The Greek Government has been operating in an atmosphere of chaos and extremism. It has made mistakes. The extension of aid by this country does not mean that the United States condones everything that the Greek Government has done or will do. We have condemned in the past, and we condemn now, extremist measures of the right or the left. We have in the past advised tolerance, and we advise tolerance now.

Turkey Also Needs Support

Greece's neighbor, Turkey, also deserves our attention.

The future of Turkey as an independent and economically sound state is clearly no less important to the freedom-loving peoples of the world than the future of Greece. The circumstances in which Turkey finds itself today are considerably different from those of Greece. Turkey has been spared the disasters that have beset Greece. And during the war, the United States and Great Britain furnished Turkey with material aid.

Nevertheless, Turkey now needs our support.

Since the war Turkey has sought additional financial assistance from Great Britain and the United States for the purpose of effecting that modernization necessary for the maintenance of its national integrity. That integrity is essential to the preservation of order in the Middle East.

The British Government has informed us that, owing to its own difficulties, it can no longer extend financial or economic aid to Turkey.

As in the case of Greece, if Turkey is to have the assistance it needs, the United States must supply it. We are the only country able to provide that help.

I am fully aware of the broad implications involved if the United States extends assistance to Greece and Turkey, and I shall discuss these implications with you at this time. One of the primary objectives of the foreign policy of the United States is the creation of conditions in which we and other nations will be able to work out a way of life free from coercion. This was a fundamental issue in the war with Germany and Japan. Our victory was won over countries which sought to impose their will, and their way of life, upon other nations.

To ensure the peaceful development of nations, free from coercion, the United States has taken a leading part in establishing the United Nations. The United Nations is designed to make possible lasting freedom and independence for all its members. We shall not realize our objectives, however, unless we are willing to help free peoples to maintain their free institutions and their national integrity against aggressive movements that seek to impose upon them totalitarian regimes.

America Must Support Democratic Efforts

This is no more than a frank recognition that totalitarian regimes imposed upon free peoples by direct or indirect aggression, undermine the foundations of international peace and hence the security of the United States.

The peoples of a number of countries of the world have recently had totalitarian regimes forced upon them against their will. The Government of the United States has made frequent protests against coercion and intimidation, in violation of the Yalta agreement, in Poland, Rumania, and Bulgaria. I must also state that in a number of other countries there have been similar developments.

At the present moment in world history nearly every nation must choose between alternative ways of life. The choice is too often not a free one.

One way of life is based upon the will of the majority, and is distinguished by free institutions, representative government, free elections, guarantees of individual liberty, freedom of speech and religion, and freedom from political oppression.

The second way of life is based upon the will of a minority forcibly imposed upon the majority. It relies upon terror and oppression, a controlled press and radio, fixed elections, and the suppression of personal freedoms.

I believe that it must be the policy of the United States to support free peoples who are resisting attempted subjugation by armed minorities or by outside pressures.

I believe that we must assist free peoples to work out their own destinies in their own way.

I believe that our help should be primarily through economic and financial aid which is essential to economic stability and orderly political processes.

The world is not static, and the *status quo* is not sacred. But we cannot allow changes in the *status quo* in violation of the Charter of the United Nations by such methods as coercion, or by such subterfuges as political infiltration. In helping free and independent nations to maintain their freedom, the United States will be giving effect to the principles of the Charter of the United Nations.

It is necessary only to glance at a map to realize that the survival and integrity of the Greek nation are of grave importance in a much wider situation. If Greece should fall under the control of an armed minority, the effect upon its neighbor, Turkey, would be immediate and serious. Confusion and disorder might well spread throughout the entire Middle East. Moreover, the disappearance of Greece as an independent state would have a profound effect upon those countries in Europe whose peoples are struggling against great difficulties to maintain their freedoms and their independence while they repair the damages of war. It would be an unspeakable tragedy if these countries, which have struggled so long against overwhelming odds, should lose that victory for which they sacrificed so much. Collapse of free institutions and loss of independence would be disastrous not only for them but for the world. Discouragement and possibly failure would quickly be the lot of neighboring peoples striving to maintain their freedom and independence.

Serious Consequences

Should we fail to aid Greece and Turkey in this fateful hour, the effect will be far reaching to the West as well as to the East.

We must take immediate and resolute action.

I therefore ask the Congress to provide authority for assistance to Greece and Turkey in the amount of $400,000,000 for the period ending June 30, 1948. In requesting these funds, I have taken into consideration the maximum amount of relief assistance which would be furnished to Greece out of the $350,000,000 which I recently requested that the Congress authorize for the prevention of starvation and suffering in countries devastated by the war. In addition to funds, I ask the Congress to authorize the detail of American civilian and military personnel to Greece and Turkey, at the request of those countries, to assist in the tasks of reconstruction, and for the purpose of supervising the use of such financial and material assistance as may be furnished. I recommend that authority also be provided for the instruction and training of selected Greek and Turkish personnel.

Finally, I ask that the Congress provide authority which will permit the speediest and most effective use, in terms of needed commodities, supplies, and equipment, of such funds as may be authorized.

If further funds, or further authority, should be needed for the purposes indicated in this message, I shall not hesitate to bring the situation before the Congress. On this subject the Executive and Legislative branches of the Government must work together.

This is a serious course upon which we embark.

I would not recommend it except that the alternative is much more serious.

The United States contributed $341,000,000,000 toward winning World War II. This is an investment in world freedom and world peace.

The assistance that I am recommending for Greece and Turkey amounts to little more than 1/10 of 1 percent of this investment.

It is only common sense that we should safeguard this investment and make sure that it was not in vain.

A Duty to Keep Hope Alive

The seeds of totalitarian regimes are nurtured by misery and want. They spread and grow in the evil soil of poverty and strife. They reach their full growth when the hope of a people for a better life has died. We must keep that hope alive.

The free peoples of the world look to us for support in maintaining their freedoms.

If we falter in our leadership, we may endanger the peace of the world—and we shall surely endanger the welfare of this Nation.

Great responsibilities have been placed upon us by the swift movement of events.

I am confident that the Congress will face these responsibilities squarely.

The Legacy of Anne Frank in the Postwar Years

by Tony Kushner

For postwar readers, the impact of Anne Frank's diary was varied. For readers who felt victorious and comfortable with the war's end, the diary was interesting and nonthreatening. For readers who felt defeated and accused at the war's end, the diary was difficult to read. Whereas some readers found redemption and hope in its pages, others found only a story with a tragic ending. Many adolescent readers found in Frank's words their own thoughts and feelings, and many adult readers saw her words as painful proof of her innocence and wasted potential. Despite the wide-ranging ways in which readers responded—and continue to respond—to Frank's diary, the fact remains that more than fifty years after its publication, the diary speaks to readers all over the world.

Tony Kushner is a lecturer, researcher, and author who specializes in Holocaust issues. In books such as *The Holocaust and the Liberal Imagination: A Social and Cultural History*, Kushner explores the historical details of Nazi persecution and power and its importance in today's world. In the following excerpt, he explains the importance of the diary to postwar readers in Europe, the United States, and Japan. He explains why Frank is such an enduring figure of the Holocaust and why she has been universalized by different groups of people.

Tony Kushner, "'I Want to Go on Living After My Death': The Memory of Anne Frank," *War and Memory in the Twentieth Century*, edited by Martin Evans and Ken Lunn. Oxford: Berg Publishers Ltd., 1997. Copyright © 1997 by Martin Evans and Ken Lunn. Reproduced by permission of the publisher.

117

*T*he Diary of Anne Frank has become the most important source of knowledge in the world today concerning the Holocaust and as Alvin Rosenfeld [*in Lessons and Legacies! The Meaning of the Holocaust in a Changing World*] points out, 'the most widely read book of World War II'. It is now seen as one of the key writings of the twentieth century, a landmark in the educational experiences of those in liberal society and more generally 'stands today, almost unrivalled, as a contemporary cultural icon'.

People Worldwide Respond to Frank

In Britain and Ireland alone well over 1 million people have visited the 'Anne Frank in the World' exhibition since it started touring in 1986. Indeed, interest in the story of Anne Frank is, if anything, growing. In 1993 it was the most popular nonfiction work in terms of library borrowing. Today her work has gained in relevance with the Bosnian disaster; thousands of British youngsters needed no prompting to see the connection when they sent parcels and letters of support to their contemporaries in former Yugoslavia after reading *The Diary*. The parallel for those in Bosnia is more than apparent:

> Our youth is very similar. After fifty years, history repeats itself in Bosnia—war, hate, killing, hiding, displacements. We are 12 years old and we can't influence politics or war, but we want to say to all the world that we want to continue our lives in freedom and peace. We wait for peace, like Anne Frank fifty years before. She didn't live to see peace, but we . . . ?

wrote the pupils of Class V13, Ivan Goran School, Zenika, Bosnia-Herzogovina in March 1993. It is clear that *The Diary of Anne Frank* loses none of its freshness to new generations in many different circumstances. This [selection] however, will concentrate on the 1950s when *The Diary*, in what was an uneven pattern, moved from obscurity to its status at the end of the decade when, as *The Times* stated, it had become 'known to millions of people all over the world'. But what did *The Diary* mean to contemporaries? How was Anne Frank interpreted just a few years after her death? Why is it that Anne Frank became such an enduring image of the Second World War to the liberal world? . . .

The [first] print run was just 1,500 and although there was enthusiasm from those whose who came into contact with *The Di-*

ary, the overall impact in the Netherlands and certainly beyond was limited. [Historian Alvin] Rosenfeld comments that these difficulties 'no doubt reflect[ed] the sense that people were tired of the war and probably did not want to be reminded all over again of the suffering that had marked the years of occupation'. Here he presents a rather generous interpretation of Dutch popular memory in the immediate post-war years. This memory was in fact selective—the misery inflicted by the German occupiers was recognized but the role played by Dutch collaborators was largely forgotten. The plight of the Jews in occupied Holland was subject to particular amnesia. Returning Jewish survivors were often treated with antipathy and sometimes open resentment. They were an unpleasant reminder of the recent past to a Dutch society experiencing an extension and perhaps an intensification of earlier antisemitic tendencies. It was especially unpleasant that this hostility was focused on the Holocaust survivors. Elie Cohen in his classic analysis *Human Behaviour in the Concentration Camps* wrote in the early 1950s that interest in the subject was 'very much on the wane'. He added that 'particularly in the Netherlands there is a notable paucity of scientific works' on the camps. There was thus little space for consideration of the difficult issues raised by *The Diary of Anne Frank. . . .*

The Diary Becomes a Best-Seller

Anne Frank has now become a symbol for all the Jews killed in the Holocaust. Until the late 1950s or early 1960s, however, the very concept of the Holocaust as a distinct historical event was not part of general popular or historical conciousness. Not even the terminology was in place. . . .

By the end of the 1950s, *The Diary*, was a best-seller everywhere, including Britain. In 1955 a Broadway play of *The Diary* was transported to Europe and a Hollywood film was released in 1959—both with immense success. As early as 1953 *The Diary* has headed sales lists in the United States and Japan. Demand for the book in Germany expanded massively in 1955 after the enormous acclaim and national trauma caused by the theatre version. Sales took off in Britain at the same time. . . .

The Japanese desperately required Anne Frank. The country's war memory was problematic in the extreme. Humiliation in defeat for what had been a martial society; the fighting of an unjust war which could not be recognized as such; and the trauma of Hiroshima and Nagasaki left a nation in need of healing and of bolstering its own self-image. Sales in Japan after its publication in 1952 were spectacular. . . . To the Japanese, Anne Frank, although European, had become an acceptable and accessible cultural figure of the war—a young victim, but one who inspired hope for the future rather than a sense of guilt for the past. Her sex further emphasized the stress on innocence, reflecting a broader trend of war representation in Japanese society. Memorials to the atomic bomb victims emphasized women and children (whilst simultaneously excluding mention of marginal groups such as the Korean immigrants who suffered massive losses). Since the 1950s *The Diary* has sold 5 million copies in Japan. . . .

Frank Becomes a Universal Figure

The reasons for the success of the book in Japan found echoes in many European countries during the 1950s. Anne Frank became universalized, she was a way of connecting to a troubled history in a non-threatening way: everyone was now a victim of the war. Whereas in Britain the book could only be marketed as one about adolescence, continental Europe (and particularly Germany) and Japan relished the book, or rather sanitized and warped versions of it, as *the* text of the Second World War. But why should it be taken to heart so quickly in the United States and why was it that by the end of the decade the dominant image of Anne Frank was American?

Sales in the United States were remarkably similar in the first year of publication to those in Japan—100,000 with the book heading the best-seller list for many weeks. Judith Doneson has written of 'the Americanization, and ultimate universalization, of the Holocaust through the *Diary*'. There is no doubt that the universal was the objective of both the award-winning Broadway play of 1955 and the film of 1959. The latter was made clear in the film company's statement that 'this isn't a Jewish picture, this is a picture for the world'. Although it was essentially Jewish writers and others who were responsible for the transformation of the diary to stage and film, there was anything but a desire to stress Jewish particularity. . . .

Frank's Diary and World War II Experiences

In conclusion, it is revealing that *The Diary of Anne Frank* is mainly referred to today in the context of Holocaust studies or the Second World War as a whole. Although general cultural histories of the post-war period give the impact of her writings no attention—in the British case writers as diverse as Alan Sinfield and Arthur Marwick have failed to mark the importance of Anne Frank—*The Diary* remains the most popular nonfiction work published since 1945. This is a serious absence in the literature because reading *The Diary of Anne Frank* was a crucial part of childhood and adolescence after the popularization of the book in the 1950s.

Excerpts from Anne Frank: The Diary of a Young Girl

by Anne Frank

Anne Marie Frank was born on June 12, 1929, in Frankfurt, Germany. It was a tumultuous time as the Great Depression in America generated a global economic and political crisis. When Adolf Hitler became Germany's chancellor in 1933, Anne's father, Otto Frank, moved his family to Amsterdam, Holland. But Holland was not far enough away. Hitler's regime occupied Holland in 1940 and enforced restrictive laws concerning Jews. As the situation worsened, Otto Frank converted an attic above his warehouse into secret living quarters for his family. In 1942 Anne's sister was called to report for labor camp registration, and the family made its move. The Franks agreed to share their hiding place with another Jewish family, the van Daans, and a dentist named Mr. Dussel.

Shortly before the Franks went into hiding, Anne received a diary for her thirteenth birthday. She named it "Kitty" and treated it as her confidante over the next two years. During this time, Anne matured from a self-conscious, melodramatic thirteen-year-old to a self-aware, insightful fifteen-year-old. She recorded her thoughts about persecution, her fear of capture, and her hopes for the future.

On August 4, 1944 (three days after Anne Frank's final diary entry), the hideaways were discovered and sent to concentration camps. Anne and her sister died of typhoid at Bergen-Belsen shortly before British troops liberated the camp. In fact, Anne's father was the only one of the eight to survive. When he returned to the hiding place, he found Anne's diary. His decision to have it published

Anne Frank, *The Diary of a Young Girl: The Definitive Edition*, edited by Otto H. Frank and Mirjam Pressler, translated by Susan Massotty. New York: Doubleday, 1995. Copyright © 1995 by Doubleday. Reproduced by permission.

changed the way millions of people think about the Holocaust.

Critics, scholars, historians, and students all over the world maintain that the enduring appeal and importance of Frank's diary is that it gives a voice to a number nobody can comprehend—6 million Jews killed in the Holocaust. To many, Frank has come to symbolize the waste and destruction of Hitler's relentless persecution of the Jews.

Wednesday, July 8, 1942

Dearest Kitty,

It seems like years since Sunday morning. So much has happened it's as if the whole world had suddenly turned upside down. But as you can see, Kitty, I'm still alive, and that's the main thing, Father says. I'm alive all right, but don't ask where or how. You probably don't understand a word I'm saying today, so I'll begin by telling you what happened Sunday afternoon.

At three o'clock . . . , the doorbell rang. I didn't hear it, since I was out on the balcony, lazily reading in the sun. A little while later Margot appeared in the kitchen doorway looking very agitated. "Father has received a call-up notice from the SS," she whispered. "Mother has gone to see Mr. van Daan" (Mr. van Daan is Father's business partner and a good friend.)

Plans to Hide from the Nazis

I was stunned. A call-up: everyone knows what that means. Visions of concentration camps and lonely cells raced through my head. How could we let Father go to such a fate? "Of course he's not going," declared Margot as we waited for Mother in the living room. "Mother's gone to Mr. van Daan to ask whether we can move to our hiding place tomorrow. The van Daans are going with us. There will be seven of us altogether."

When she and I were sitting in our bedroom, Margot told me that the call-up was not for Father, but for her. At this second shock, I began to cry. Margot is sixteen—apparently they want to send girls her age away on their own. But thank goodness she won't be going; Mother had said so herself, which must be what Father had meant when he talked to me about our going into hiding. Hiding . . . where would we hide? In the city? In the country? In a house? In a shack? When, where, how . . .? These were questions I wasn't allowed to ask, but they still kept running through my mind.

Margot and I started packing our most important belongings into a schoolbag. The first thing I stuck in was this diary, and then curlers, handkerchiefs, schoolbooks, a comb and some old letters. Preoccupied by the thought of going into hiding, I stuck the craziest things in the bag, but I'm not sorry. Memories mean more to me than dresses. . . .

News from the Outside

Friday, October 9, 1942

Dearest Kitty,

Today I have nothing but dismal and depressing news to report. Our many Jewish friends and acquaintances are being taken away in droves. The Gestapo is treating them very roughly and transporting them in cattle cars to Westerbork, the big camp in Drenthe to which they're sending all the Jews. Miep [Gies, one of their outside contacts] told us about someone who'd managed to escape from there. It must be terrible in Westerbork. The people get almost nothing to eat, much less to drink, as water is available only one hour a day, and there's only one toilet and sink for several thousand people. Men and women sleep in the same room, and women and children often have their heads shaved. Escape is almost impossible; many people look Jewish, and they're branded by their shorn heads.

If it's that bad in Holland, what must it be like in those faraway and uncivilized places where the Germans are sending them? We assume that most of them are being murdered. The English radio says they're being gassed. Perhaps that's the quickest way to die.

I feel terrible. Miep's accounts of these horrors are so heart-rending, and Miep is also very distraught. The other day, for instance, the Gestapo deposited an elderly, crippled Jewish woman on Miep's doorstep while they set off to find a car. The old woman was terrified of the glaring searchlights and the guns firing at the English planes overhead. Yet Miep didn't dare let her in. Nobody would. The Germans are generous enough when it comes to punishment.

Bep [another outside contact] is also very subdued. Her boyfriend is being sent to Germany. Every time the planes fly over, she's afraid they're going to drop their entire bomb load on Bertus's head. Jokes like "Oh, don't worry, they can't all fall on him" or "One bomb is all it takes" are hardly appropriate in this situation. Bertus is not the only one being forced to work in Germany. Trainloads of young men depart daily. Some of them try to sneak off the train when it stops at a small station, but only a few manage to escape unnoticed and find a place to hide.

The Persecution of Suspected Traitors

But that's not the end of my lamentations. Have you ever heard the term "hostages"? That's the latest punishment for saboteurs. It's the most horrible thing you can imagine. Leading citizens— innocent people—are taken prisoner to await their execution. If the Gestapo can't find the saboteur, they simply grab five hostages

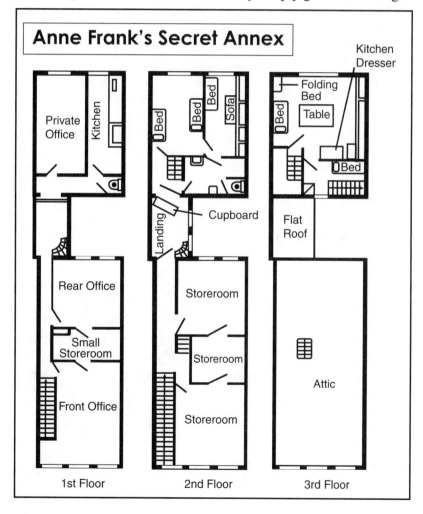

and line them up against the wall. You read the announcements of their death in the paper, where they're referred to as "fatal accidents."

Fine specimens of humanity, those Germans, and to think I'm actually one of them! No, that's not true, Hitler took away our nationality long ago. And besides, there are no greater enemies on earth than the Germans and the Jews.

Yours, Anne. . .

Terrified of Being Found

Thursday, March 25, 1943

Dearest Kitty,

Mother, Father, Margot and I were sitting quite pleasantly together last night when Peter suddenly came in and whispered in Father's ear. I caught the words "a barrel falling over in the warehouse" and "someone fiddling with the door."

Margot heard it too, but was trying to calm me down, since I'd turned white as chalk and was extremely nervous. The three of us waited while Father and Peter went downstairs. A minute or two later Mrs. van Daan came up from where she'd been listening to the radio and told us that Pim [Otto Frank] had asked her to turn it off and tiptoe upstairs. But you know what happens when you're trying to be quiet—the old stairs creaked twice as loud. Five minutes later Peter and Pim, the color drained from their faces, appeared again to relate their experiences.

They had positioned themselves under the staircase and waited. Nothing happened. Then all of a sudden they heard a couple of bangs, as if two doors had been slammed shut inside the house. Pim bounded up the stairs, while Peter went to warn Dussel, who finally presented himself upstairs, though not without kicking up a fuss and making a lot of noise. Then we all tiptoed in our stockinged feet to the van Daans on the next floor. Mr. van D. had a bad cold and had already gone to bed, so we gathered around his bedside and discussed our suspicions in a whisper. Every time Mr. van D. coughed loudly, Mrs. van D. and I nearly had a nervous fit. He kept coughing until someone came up with the bright idea of giving him codeine. His cough subsided immediately.

Once again we waited and waited, but heard nothing. Finally we came to the conclusion that the burglars had taken to their heels when they heard footsteps in an otherwise quiet building.

The problem now was that the chairs in the private office were neatly grouped around the radio, which was tuned to England. If the burglars had forced the door and the air-raid wardens were to notice it and call the police, there could be very serious repercussions. So Mr. van Daan got up, pulled on his coat and pants, put on his hat and cautiously followed Father down the stairs, with Peter (armed with a heavy hammer, to be on the safe side) right behind him. The ladies (including Margot and me) waited in suspense until the men returned five minutes later and reported that there was no sign of any activity in the building. . . .

If you're wondering whether it's harder for the adults here than for the children, the answer is no, it's certainly not. Older people have an opinion about everything and are sure of themselves and their actions. It's twice as hard for us young people to hold on to our opinions at a time when ideals are being shattered and destroyed, when the worst side of human nature predominates, when everyone has come to doubt truth, justice and God.

Anyone who claims that the older folks have a more difficult time in the Annex doesn't realize that the problems have a far greater impact on *us*. We're much too young to deal with these problems, but they keep thrusting themselves on us until, finally, we're forced to think up a solution, though most of the time our solutions crumble when faced with the facts. It's difficult in times like these: ideals, dreams and cherished hopes rise within us, only to be crushed by grim reality. It's a wonder I haven't abandoned all my ideals, they seem so absurd and impractical. Yet I cling to them because I still believe, in spite of everything, that people are truly good at heart.

It's utterly impossible for me to build my life on a foundation of chaos, suffering and death. I see the world being slowly transformed into a wilderness, I hear the approaching thunder that, one day, will destroy us too, I feel the suffering of millions. And yet, when I look up at the sky, I somehow feel that everything will change for the better, that this cruelty too shall end, that peace and tranquility will return once more. In the meantime, I must hold on to my ideals. Perhaps the day will come when I'll be able to realize them!

Yours, Anne M. Frank

The People's Republic of China Is Established:
October 1, 1949

The Chinese Revolution and Communism in China

by John E. Schrecker

The Chinese civil war began during the 1930s between the Nationalists led by Chiang Kai-shek and the Communists led by Mao Zedong (also spelled Tse-tung). Although World War II temporarily halted the civil war, it resumed after Japan surrendered to the Allies. In 1946 and early 1947, the Nationalists were leading until Mao's forces suddenly overpowered them in Manchuria during the summer of 1947. The Nationalists lost ground quickly and began surrendering in September 1948. Fortified by their strong position, the Communists ceased negotiations, and on October 1, 1949, Mao announced the formation of the People's Republic of China. The Nationalists fled to Formosa (now Taiwan), where Chiang Kai-shek maintained that he was the rightful ruler of China. The presence of two factions in China with two leaders claiming authority created problems domestically and internationally. Nations dealing with China had to choose which government they acknowledged as being official. Mao and the Communists, however, controlled all the land and population, with the exception of Formosa.

Mao soon aligned his republic with the Soviet Union. Because this meant mutual military support for communism in Europe and now China, this alliance officially ushered the Cold War into eastern Asia. The balance of power in the world dramatically shifted when

China became a Communist nation, and its stature would later be influential in the Korean War.

John E. Schrecker is a history professor at Brandeis University. His expertise in the area of Chinese studies and intercultural history has not only earned him membership in the Fairbank Center for East Asian Research at Harvard, but it has also led him to write *The Chinese Revolution in Historical Perspective* and *Imperialism and Chinese Nationalism*. In the following excerpt, Schrecker describes what life was like inside China in the years following the establishment of Communist rule.

S ince 1949, China, after a thousand years of the junxian [a Chinese social model with a centralized government] system, has been in a new phase of her history. As a result, using the past to clarify the present, the only means available, is particularly uncertain. At the same time, the difficulties of obtaining sound information are increased by the fact that for the past forty years Chinese society has been tightly controlled, and much that is significant and interesting has been unavailable to the Chinese people, let alone to foreigners. Finally, problems of objectivity are increased for Americans because for many years the United States and China had very poor relations, and the two nations still have profound political differences. Dogmatism is always out of place in understanding humankind and never more so than in the study of contemporary China.

A New Order in China

When Mao Zedong proclaimed the establishment of the People's Republic of China, he had the active support of a vast number of his fellow citizens, the enthusiastic sympathy of even more, and the guarded hopes and well wishes of almost everyone else. The new government was the product of 150 years of revolutionary activity that had found increasing favor in the eyes of the Chinese people and of moral idealism and political opposition that dated back far earlier. At the same time, the Communist leadership seemed deeply committed to solving the problems that had fueled discontent for so long and that had, in many ways, become even worse in the years since the fall of the Qing [dynasty]: poverty, unrepresentative and ineffective government, national weakness, and a poor moral climate.

In facing these mammoth tasks, the new government not only had the benefit of historical ideals and the support of the Chinese people but also had the organizational strength of the Communist Party and the experience that it had garnered in the revolutionary struggles of the previous thirty years. At the same time, the leaders had the zeal and self-confidence that came from Marxism's faith in the inevitability of progress and the possibilities of creating a just and prosperous society.

On the other hand, they were also burdened by attitudes that had caused problems in the past and would become even more serious in the future. Thus, the authoritarian legacies of the junxian age and the pressing problems of the nation combined with Marxist-Leninist dogma to encourage dictatorial rule. In particular, the notion that China had just emerged from fengjian [a Chinese social model with a decentralized government] and had an unsophisticated population of "peasants" provided a poor framework for appreciating the full capacities and commitment of the Chinese people. In addition, since the Communists still found little or no value in Chinese history or philosophy, they compounded the problems of entering a new era and reconstructing the social system by separating themselves from the viewpoints most appropriate to their needs: China's own traditions and, in particular, the radical thought of the junxian age and the "socialist" theories embodied in the datong [concept of an ideal society] approach.

The overall result of this situation has been that from the vantage of both social justice and economic development, the People's Republic has made some progress on the tasks it faced forty years ago. At the same time, however, it has also experienced failures, many of great magnitude. Over time, policies have developed that have sometimes seemed to be more in harmony with Chinese possibilities and Chinese realities. However, the process has barely begun, and most observers would agree that today the Chinese government and the Communist Party find themselves in deep trouble.

Emulating the Soviet Union

The first five years of Communist rule in China were devoted primarily to establishing an effective political system. There were also considerable concern and comparative success in improving public welfare and beginning economic growth. It was an era in which China came under heavy Soviet influence and also fought the United States in Korea. Overall, these early years did much to establish the structure and set the tone for the subsequent history of the People's Republic.

In the Yenan [from the mid-1930s to the mid-1940s] years, Chinese communism had been comparatively free of foreign influences, if not in theory, at least to a considerable degree in practice. With the establishment of the People's Republic, however, Mao Zedong proclaimed a renewed dedication to the Soviet Union as China's "teacher" in socialism. At the same time, he said that the new government would "lean to one side" in international affairs in favor of Russia and the Eastern bloc. On the broadest level, the reason for this approach was that Russia was the most powerful nation in the world that proclaimed itself to be a Marxist-Leninist state. In the 1920s the Chinese Communists had copied Russian models because they suggested techniques for a successful revolution; now, Russia appeared to hold the clue on how to create and develop a socialist society.

More specifically, Soviet national practice stressed things that were particularly crucial in the early years of the Communist ascendancy: political order and economic development. At the same time, Russia, fresh from her victories in the Second World War, seemed to indicate how a socialist country could maintain her national security in a hostile world. Finally, direct Russian aid, both for economic development and as an ally in international affairs, required that China emulate the Soviet Union, for the latter, in the theocratic style of Marxism-Leninism, required Communist countries to follow and, indeed, to fawn over the political organization and socioeconomic theories.

Once in power, the Chinese Communists were able to reestablish a stable political system quickly and with comparative ease. This achievement was partly a tribute to their own political skills and sense of organization as well as to the long-standing Chinese traditions of political unity and to the thirst for order after several generations of chaos and war. The system that was established was, essentially, a highly centralized dictatorship of the Communist Party. This sort of rule was not, of course, in line with the datong ideals that had influenced the revolution in its pre-Communist phase and that aimed at enhancing democracy and replacing the excessive centralization of the junxian system with the decentralized benefits of fengjian. However, the system reflected both the immediate need for national order and the Soviet example. . . .

By 1949, the Communist Party, the core of the system, had four to five million members. As usual, we do not have a good statistical study of the group's social composition. However, it seems to have included a fair representation of the broad coalition that had carried out the revolution. Party membership was considered to be a great honor and was avidly sought. Cadres were expected to keep a high tone of commitment and selfless devotion to society, and repeated "rectification campaigns" and educational drives were carried out to ensure that they would remain so.

Officially, the party was organized democratically through a series of elections from the lowest units up to the top, the Central Committee and its Standing Committee and, supreme over all, the Political Bureau (Politburo), a group of about ten people who stood at the zenith of the system. In practice, however, power and decision making moved from the top downward rather than from the bottom up. The Politburo and its undisputed head, Mao Zedong, ran things. Below them, orders and even slates of candidates came from one level to the one beneath. Those on a lower rung had precious little input into policy, and public criticism of those in control, in particular of the Politburo, was not permitted.

The Communist Party ran the government and society in much the same way as Mao Zedong and the Politburo ran the party; the official structure was democratic, but the practice was highly regimented. In theory, the government was made up of a coalition composed of a number of political parties, a system that aimed at giving expression to the broad support that the revolution had received. In Communist jargon, China was a "Dictatorship of the People" rather than a "Dictatorship of the Proletariat" as existed in Russia where only the Communist Party was permitted. At the same time, governmental power was supposed to pass upward through various levels to a parliament, the National People's Congress, which was established as the highest political organ of the state.

In reality, however, the Communist Party was completely dominant; all aspects of political life were under its control, and orders moved outward from it to the rest of society. People did not feel free to criticize party members, and no real opposition was permitted to exist. To cement the system and his own power, Mao Zedong established himself as chief of state as well as chairman of the party. During the Communists' rise to power something of a cult of personality had begun to develop around the chairman. Now this grew apace, and official propaganda rarely missed a chance to speak in glowing terms of Mao's leadership and of his pivotal role in Chinese life. . . .

The Communist Reign of Terror

For those suspected of posing a threat to the system or of being in serious opposition to it, punishment was extremely severe. In the late 1940s and early 1950s, many of the former elite in the rural areas were denounced and tried; many were executed. In the cities there were several campaigns aimed at ferreting out "counter-revolutionaries," and there was also much killing. We do not have figures on the total number of people who died, but Mao himself admitted to at least one million executions, and sober foreign estimates have run as high as five million.

Those killed were generally accused of being local tyrants or of having collaborated with the Japanese during the war. Nonetheless, there is evidence that the average person was able to understand the crimes involved as products of the tragic and competitive atmosphere of the previous decades. As a result, party cadres, acting on orders from above, often had to stage manage trials and arouse people to mete out punishment. In a sense, then, the mass killings of these early years were not only terrible in their own right, but also represent a further example of political manipulation, of the fear that the Chinese people were too unsophisticated to reeducate and assimilate those who disagreed or might disagree with the new society, however powerless they had become.

China Enters the Korean War

One thing that bolstered the dictatorial tendencies of the time and also China's reliance on the Soviet Union was the Korean War. The United States became involved in Korea in June 1950 and by the autumn of that year was beginning to carry the war to the northern, Communist portion of the divided nation, territory directly adjacent to China's Manchurian provinces. Peking, with its government barely in place and with memories of imperialism fresh in its consciousness, felt threatened and issued repeated warnings against further American moves toward the border. These went unheeded, however, and in October, China entered the conflict on the northern side. An unofficial but bloody war ensued, which lasted for three years and in which Russia gave considerable aid to China.

In America, it should be noted, the Korean War generated intense hostility toward the new government in China. The United States became the guardians of the Kuomintang regime on Taiwan and continued to recognize it rather than Peking as the legitimate government of China. At the same time, the United States worked to isolate Peking on the international scene and to make certain that Taiwan represented the country in the United Nations and in other international activities, such as the Olympics. Taiwan retained China's seat in the UN until 1971, and the United States did not begin a rapprochement until the next year, finally recognizing the legitimacy of the People's Republic in 1979. American policy and China's exclusion from the world community were probably the most vivid and galling reminders of the imperialist era during the first decades of the People's Republic.

The Communist Government Addresses Domestic Problems

Once unity and order had been restored, the new government began to deal with China's other problems. The most striking advances were in the field of public welfare and in the status of women, areas where the injustices of the past had done much to fuel the revolution and where the reestablishment of effective government coupled with Communist ideology could achieve rapid but fundamental improvements.

The Communists made a concerted effort to alleviate the endemic want and misery that had plagued the nation for so long, to give people some security and a sense of possibility for the future. Most importantly, they worked effectively to ensure that everyone had the basic necessities of life. As a result, though the nation remained extremely poor, the mass degradation of the previous century and a half became, for the most part, a thing of the past. In addition, the Communists worked to reestablish a broadly based system of schools and, thereby, began a major improvement in the educational levels of the average person for the first time since the eighteenth century. Finally, the government put much effort into medical care and initiated the foundations of a national system of public health.

At the same time, the new regime was deeply concerned to end discrimination against women. The role that women played in the Communist Party and in various mass organizations gave them a greater public power than they had ever enjoyed before. Soon new marriage laws began to work against injustices in private life. Needless to say, foot binding, which had been in decline since early in the century, came to a complete halt. On paper, then, women were set on the path of full parity with men. In many aspects of life this equality has remained rather theoretical, as it has in all societies, even those committed to the full emancipation of women. However, in China, achievements in women's rights have been immense, particularly in comparison to the junxian past, and the progress that has occurred may, in the number of people it has directly affected, be accounted the greatest improvement that the destruction of the old order has brought to society.

Despite their concern with improving public welfare, there was one major aspect of the task that the Communists chose to ignore, the question of population control. China's huge population was the product of the nation's extended and prosperous junxian age. The number of people had declined in times of chaos but had doubled during each era of dynastic stability, leaving a legacy of half a billion to the People's Republic. . . .

Peking virtually ignored the issue of overpopulation until the 1970s. By then China had a billion people, and the resulting problems were felt in every area of life. In the long view, neglecting demographic pressures may prove to have been the most serious mistake in the early history of the People's Republic.

Communism Was Expected to Modernize China

The basic advances in human welfare begun by the new government rested on good order, commitment, and utilizing China's existing economic base to the utmost. Sustained progress, particularly as the population continued to grow, however, required the introduction and application of contemporary industrial and scientific techniques to economic life. In the previous hundred years, all efforts at comprehensive and sustained development had failed. As a result, the hope that socialism would make modernization possible and, thereby, overcome the nation's poverty and military weakness was also a key factor in the revolution; from the beginning, the Communists considered it to be one of their prime tasks. . . .

In line with the Stalinist plan, the government quickly began to collectivize the economy and to establish control over it. In Soviet fashion, a five-year plan was promulgated to coordinate activities and set targets for growth. Industry and commerce were brought under Peking's direction. Many enterprises were nationalized. In others, the original owners continued in possession, though only on paper. In practice they became government employees, and all remnants of private enterprise were understood as temporary expedients, a compromise with socialism.

Similarly, agriculture also moved steadily toward collectivization to accord with socialist ideals as well as to increase production and to tax farmers more effectively. In Russia in the 1930s, collectivization had been a highly coercive and bloody process. Though there were problems in China, the process went far more smoothly. The chief reason seems to have been that the competitiveness, inequalities, and insecurity of the junxian land system, problems that had long fueled the opposition and that had contributed to the socialist thrust of the revolution, now made Chinese farmers more receptive to collective ownership than were those in Russia, with its recent fengjian past. In addition, despite their Marxist-Leninist prejudices, the Chinese Communists had far more powerful roots in a rural constituency than did their Russian counterparts. . . .

The Stalinist Model Yields Results

Given the problems that China had experienced in recent centuries with economic development, the Stalinist Model was put into effect with considerable success. During the five-year plan, the national rate of savings, that is, the amount of money put aside for investment on a national basis, seems to have been comparable to the high rates that the Soviet Union achieved in the 1930s. This rate was particularly remarkable in view of the fact that China had a lower per capita income than had Russia, and so there was less surplus available for investment after the people's basic needs were met.

As the capital thus accumulated began to be used, China showed a rapid rise in the GNP [gross national product]. The major part of the rise, of course, came in industry and especially in heavy industry. Most of this was in the form of electric power for factories, the extraction and processing of minerals and petroleum, and the production of machinery. By 1958, China was a major industrial power in terms of total output (though not, of course, in per capita production), perhaps one of the top ten nations in the world.

Agriculture grew also, though, as one would expect given the development plan, far more slowly. Unlike industry, this rise did not come about through new investment, for which the five-year plan made few provisions. Rather it was basically a result of the greater sense of justice and security that the Communists brought to rural areas. In addition, it rested on increased efficiency in the coordination and application of labor power, both in the fields and for various large-scale projects, such as improvements in water control. The rise in agricultural production was, of course, central to the gains in industry. The farms provided not only much of the capital for growth but also food for the growing number of people in manufacturing. At the same time, the crucial imports of industrial equipment that China did not yet make were paid for through the export of agricultural goods.

The Tortuous Search for a Chinese Way

By the mid-fifties, then, the Chinese government, though dictatorial and dogmatic, seemed to be making significant headway in dealing with the nation's most pressing problems. At this time, however, Mao Zedong and the Communist leaders began to see difficulties in the way things were progressing and initiated changes in policy that were to signal a new era in the history of the People's Republic. Essentially, they began to move the nation away from Soviet models.

In the long run, as had been the case earlier at Yenan, this shift signaled the possibility of using China's own heritage and the good sense and commitment of its people as the basis of political life, economic growth, and the construction of socialism. In practice, however, the new approaches continued to be plagued by the deep alienation from the past and all its works that had originally inspired the May 4th generation [the group of revolutionaries who sought a new system of government], the group that still dominated the country. Similarly, the new policies still reflected the intolerant sectarianism of Marxism-Leninism and, in particular, the view that the average citizen of China, the heir of an irretrievably useless and backward past, was deeply prone to error unless properly led.

As a result, the innovations of the late fifties failed for the most part, leaving even greater problems in their wake. At the same time, they opened the way to an increase in the dictatorial authority of those who ruled the country; for if guidelines to action now came neither from Russian models nor from the Chinese

past and if the Chinese people were not sophisticated and progressive but simply "poor and blank," as Mao Zedong said in
these years, then success depended more than ever on the unique
insights and wisdom of the Communist Party and, in particular,
on Mao himself. . . .

Critics of the New Regime Become Vocal

In response to the weaknesses of the first years of the Communist regime, the elite produced a flood of criticism and a wealth
of new ideas. Like most people in China, almost all of them had
supported the revolution, and a not insignificant number had even
returned from abroad in 1949 to help their nation in what they
hoped would be its moment of rebirth. As a result, there were almost no attacks on the general goal of socialism nor calls for a
return to old and discredited ways of doing things. Nonetheless,
the suggestions for change were often broad and fundamental.
The critics not only proposed alternatives to this or that particular policy, including suggestions for investment in agriculture and
for a vigorous policy of birth control, but also attacked the dictatorial character of Communist rule. . . .

Nonetheless, Mao Zedong and the party leaders launched a
sharp swing away from open discussion and disagreement. By
1957, what remained of the Hundred Flowers Movement [a 1956
effort to improve the political scene] was brought to a halt and
replaced by a harsh and unjust "Anti-Rightist Campaign." Those
who had made criticisms or suggested new policies were denounced as reactionary and antisocialist. Many were imprisoned,
sent to labor camps, or suffered the loss of their jobs. Eventually,
Mao made matters worse by claiming that he had started the
Hundred Flowers Campaign only to uncover secret opponents of
socialism, dangerous and poisonous weeds. Like Stalin before
him, Mao, it seemed, would rather be thought a cynical tyrant
than to admit that he had made errors in policy or in his estima-
tion of the opposition to them.

The retreat from the Hundred Flowers Campaign proved to be
the beginning of a great and sustained tragedy for the People's Republic that was to encompass much of the next twenty years. . . .

Mao Initiates the Cultural Revolution

It was Mao Zedong, who had played such a leading role in the
construction of the existing order, who led the search for politi-

cal renovation [during the early 1960s]. The results were to prove as tragic as anything that had yet occurred in the People's Republic. Approaching his seventy-fifth year and in failing health, Mao became obsessed by the fact that the socialist society of which he had dreamed and for which he had fought was being permanently foreclosed by the formation of a new elite. Surprisingly, coming from him, he indicated that this elite was lodged in the Communist Party, indeed, that essentially it was the Communist Party. He decided that the party and its leaders were turning into a closed group whose only interest was maintaining itself in power and, perhaps, supplying some short-term economic gains.

Though Mao's concerns were, in many ways, more than justifiable, his response to them was still fraught with all the disrespect for Chinese history and with all the zeal and dogmatism that had influenced the thinking of his generation for so long. As a result he did not put his immense prestige and political skills behind a call for the genuine democracy that alone could permanently limit the power of the party, for he still mistrusted the Chinese people to create a good society in an atmosphere of calm and deliberation.

Rather, Mao used his power to initiate a bizarre replay of the May 4th Movement: The Great Proletarian Cultural Revolution. Thus, he decided to reconstruct China from the ground up once again. This time, however, the goal would be to free the culture not only from the evils of the Chinese past but also from the shortcomings that he had begun to sense, if only unconsciously, in Western outlooks and, in particular in Marxism-Leninism. Mao decided, further, to accomplish this goal, by utilizing the same group that had led the May 4th Movement: the youth. . . .

Since the ideology behind the Cultural Revolution saw no strengths in Chinese tradition and precious few in the practice of Marxism-Leninism, its only basis could be the thought of Mao Zedong himself. As a result, to stimulate the Red Guards to action, Mao encouraged an unprecedented cult of personality centered on himself and his infallible wisdom. The most famous symbol of the cult became the *Selected Quotations from Mao Zedong*, the so-called Little Red Book, which was printed and distributed in over a billion copies and became a talisman for overcoming all obstacles.

Once goaded on by such authority, the youth proved zealous.

In addition to the propaganda urging them forward, they were also stimulated by the fact that the educational advances of the previous decade had left a larger group of talented and trained young people than could be accommodated by China's still relatively backward economy. At the same time, schools closed down. Shutting the schools was tied to the fact that they were, for the most part, under party control and also said to be unfairly biased toward the elite. However, the basic reason they were closed, aside from freeing the young for political activism, was to promote the idea that there was nothing worth teaching, either in China's long-term past or in her recent Communist heritage.

In this nihilistic atmosphere the youth and the older people who decided to go along with them, either out of fear or self-interest, began attacks on everything from music to the organization of factories. Cultural treasures, buildings, and artworks were defaced and sometimes destroyed. Industrial production declined. Most seriously, however, the followers of the Cultural Revolution began widespread abuse of party members, intellectuals, and social leaders of all sorts.

It was a time of humiliation, beatings, killings, and suicides, and those who died may have numbered up to half a million. Ever more people were sent to prisons and work camps. . . .

China Today

After the death of Mao Zedong [in 1976] and the end of the Cultural Revolution, the Communist Party resumed control of China and in the succeeding years has continued the general tendency begun in the late 1950s to find an appropriately Chinese approach to national affairs. As compared to the previous twenty years, there has been some progress. But, overall, the results remain extremely mixed, and China still seems far from having found her own way to a successful and healthy society.

10 Rosa Parks Refuses to Surrender Her Bus Seat: December 1, 1955

Parks's Refusal Initiated a History-Making Boycott

by David Halberstam

Many Americans associate the civil rights movement with the 1960s, but it had strong roots in the mid-1950s. In the South, racial segregation was a way of life, and there were pervasive social rules for interaction between the races. Some whites were not afraid to challenge the rules by treating blacks as equals, but many more were quite content maintaining separation between themselves and blacks. Schools, buses, public rest rooms and water fountains, and housing areas were segregated by race. Segregation was not just the result of old habits, it was the law.

Two important strides for equal rights came in 1954 and 1955. In 1954 the Supreme Court handed down its decision in the case of *Brown v. Board of Education*, a decision that overturned the "separate-but-equal" doctrine of a previous case, *Plessy v. Ferguson* (1896). This doctrine stated that keeping the races segregated was constitutional as long as facilities were equal. In *Brown v. Board of Education*, the judges ruled that this idea was impossible and that school segregation was no longer legal. The backlash was so severe that President Dwight D. Eisenhower sent U.S. Army troops to Little Rock, Arkansas, to ensure the safety of black students arriving for the first time to a previously all-white school.

The next year, 1955, a woman named Rosa Parks refused to surrender her bus seat to a white man, even though the law dictated that blacks had to give up their seats to any white that boarded.

David Halberstam, *The Fifties*. New York: Villard Books, 1993. Copyright © 1993 by The Amateurs Limited. Reproduced by permission.

Parks was an activist and admits that she kept the seat not so much because she was physically tired as because she was emotionally tired of the poor treatment of blacks. Police arrested Parks, leading to an organized bus boycott in Montgomery, Alabama, which threatened to bankrupt the bus lines when their income decreased by 75 percent. On December 21, 1956, the Supreme Court declared that racial segregation on buses was unconstitutional. This marked important victory for civil rights as another social door opened to blacks. It was also important because it showed that people seemingly stripped of power could make changes in their society through nonviolent means.

The Montgomery bus boycott was also important because it was the first cause taken up by a new black leader, Martin Luther King Jr. During the late 1950s and 1960s, King was arguably the most high-profile leader in the civil rights movement. He advocated equality, fairness, and goodwill by use of nonviolent means. His sudden death by an assassin's bullet remains one of the saddest moments of the twentieth century.

Pulitzer Prize–winning journalist David Halberstam is the author of numerous books about modern American history written for mainstream readers. His wide-ranging subjects include Manhattan firefighters on September 11, 2001 *(Firehouse)*, the Vietnam War *(The Best and the Brightest)*, amateur rowing *(The Amateurs)*, and the modern media *(The Powers That Be)*. In the following excerpt, he relates the events of the historic Montgomery bus boycott.

On the evening of December 1, 1955, Mrs. Rosa Parks's entire body ached—her feet, neck, and shoulders were especially sore. Parks was a tailor's assistant in a Montgomery, Alabama, department store. Hers was an exhausting job that paid a minimal salary; she made alterations and had to handle a large commercial steam press as well. On this particular day, she finished work and walked a few blocks as usual to the bus stop. The first bus on her route was so crowded she realized that there would be no place left to sit, and she desperately needed to get off her feet. She decided to wait for a less crowded bus. That gave her a little time to waste, so Parks walked over to a nearby drugstore to look for a heating pad, which might help ease the pain in her sore muscles. Not finding anything to her liking, she returned to the bus stop. Eventually, a bus arrived that had a fair number of seats available. She paid her ten cents, boarded the bus, and took a seat in the rear, or black, section of the bus, near the dividing line between the white and black sections. On Montgomery's public buses, the first ten rows were for white people, the last twenty-six for blacks. In many cities in the South, the line dividing sections on buses was fixed. This was not true in Montgomery; by custom, the driver had the power, if need be, to expand the white section and shrink the black section by ordering blacks to give up their seats to whites. First come, first served might have been the rule of public transportation in most of America, but it was not true in Montgomery, Alabama, in 1955. To the blacks, it was just one additional humiliation to be suffered—because the system did not even guarantee the minimal courtesies and rights of traditional segregation.

Three other blacks boarded the bus and sat next to Mrs. Parks in the same row. Parks had already recognized the driver as one of the meaner-spirited white men who worked for the bus line. He had once evicted her from his bus because she had refused, on paying her fare, to leave the bus and reenter the black section from the rear door—another quaint custom inflicted on black Montgomery bus riders. Gradually, as the bus continued on its rounds more whites got on. Finally, with the white section filled, a white man boarded. The driver, J.F. Blake, turned to look behind him at the first row of blacks and said, "You let him have those front seats." That was not a suggestion, it was an order. It meant that not only did one seat have to be freed, but the other three blacks would have to move as well, lest the white man have to sit next to a black. All four blacks knew what Blake meant, but no one moved. Blake looked behind him again and added, "You all better make it light on yourselves and let me have those seats." The three other blacks reluctantly got up and moved toward the back. Rosa Parks did not. She was frightened, but she was tired. She did not want to give up her seat, and she most certainly did not want to stand up the rest of the way. She had just spent her entire day working in a department store tailoring and pressing clothes for white people and now she was being told that she had no rights.

Parks Is Arrested

"Look, woman, I told you I wanted the seat. Are you going to stand up?" Blake said. Finally, Rosa Parks spoke. "No," she said.

"If you don't stand up, I'm going to have you arrested," Blake warned her. She told him to go right ahead, but she was not going to move.

Blake got off the bus and went to phone the police, thereby involuntarily entering the nation's history books; his was the most ordinary example of a Southern white man fending off any threat to the system of segregation. If it had not been Blake, it would have been someone else. Some of the black riders, sensing trouble, or possibly irritated by the delay, started getting off the bus.

Parks continued to sit. In so doing she became the first prominent figure of what became the Movement. Perhaps the most interesting thing about her was how ordinary she was, at least on the surface, almost the prototype of the black women who toiled so hard and had so little to show for it. She had not, she later explained, thought about getting arrested that day. Later, the stunned white leaders of Montgomery repeatedly charged that Parks's refusal was part of a carefully orchestrated plan on the part of the local NAACP, of which she was an officer. But that was not true; what she did represented one person's exhaustion with a system that dehumanized all black people. Something inside her finally snapped. But if she had not planned to resist on that particular day, then it was also true that Rosa Parks had decided some time earlier that if she was ever asked to give up her seat for a white person, she would refuse to do so.

Rosa Parks was often described in newspaper reports as merely a seamstress, but she was more than that; she was a person of unusual dignity and uncommon strength of character. . . .

As the bus driver continued to shout at her, Parks thought to herself, how odd it was that you go through life making things comfortable for white people yet they don't even treat you like a human being. There was something inevitable about this confrontation—a collision of rising black expectations with growing white resistance. At that moment in Montgomery, as in most deep South cities, school integration was still an abstract concept, something that had not yet happened and was not near happening. By contrast, riding a bus was the flashpoint, the center of daily, bitterly resented abuse.

Soon two Montgomery policemen arrived. Was it true that the driver had asked her to get up? they asked. Yes, she said. Why hadn't she obeyed? She felt she shouldn't have to. "Why do you push us around?" she asked. "I don't know, but the law is the law, and you're under arrest," one of the policemen said. Only then did she get up. The police escorted her to the patrol car. The police went back to talk to Blake. Did he want to press charges? Yes, he answered. The police took Parks to jail, where she was fingerprinted and charged with violating the city's segregation laws. She was allowed one phone call, and she called her home. Her mother answered and asked instinctively, "Did they beat you?" No, she said, she was physically all right. She was the first person ever so charged—the first of many tactical mistakes on the part of city officials, for it gave the local black community what it had been seeking: the case on which to hang a lawsuit.

After her phone call home, the news of her arrest spread quickly through the black community. Edgar D. Nixon, Parks's friend, called the police station to find out what had happened. Nixon was a Pullman car porter, a union man, and a powerful presence in the black community. For some twenty years he had been a black leader and activist in a town that despised the idea of racial change, and he became, in the process, absolutely fearless. There might be some blacks who did not like him, but

Rosa Parks is fingerprinted after being arrested for refusing to give up her bus seat to a white man.

everyone respected him, including some of the white leadership. For more than a decade, he had engaged in one of the most dangerous tasks of all—trying to register blacks to vote. On occasion, he did it carrying a shotgun under his coat. When Nixon called the police station to inquire about Rosa Parks, he was told it was none of his business. So he telephoned Clifford Durr [a friend and the employer of Parks], who said he would post bond. Nixon was not displeased by what had happened: This was the case he had been looking for. Mrs. Parks was the perfect defendant: She had worked with him in the NAACP for twelve years, and he knew she was a strong, confident person. If she said she was going to do something, she did it, and no amount of pressure from the white community would deter her. Her example would most likely give strength to others nervous about challenging the white establishment.

Parks's Story Prompts a Bus Boycott

That night Parks, her family, the Durrs, and Ed Nixon sat around to discuss the details of her case. Nixon badly wanted to use it to test the constitutionality of the bus law. Would she agree, he asked, to be a test case? The idea frightened Raymond Parks, her husband, a local barber who knew the violence that traditionally awaited those blacks foolhardy enough to challenge the system. He warned her, "Oh, the white folks will kill you, Rosa. Don't do anything to make trouble, Rosa. Don't bring a suit. The whites will kill you." She was torn. She did not want to put her family at risk, but neither did she want herself or the younger black people who came after her to face such indignities. Nor did she want to face them anymore herself. "If you think we can get anywhere with it, I'll go along with it," she told Nixon.

Nixon went home and sketched a map of Montgomery—where blacks lived and where they worked. The distances were not, he decided, insurmountable. "You know what?" he told his wife.

"What?" she asked.

"We're going to boycott the buses," he said.

"Cold as it is?" she answered skeptically.

"Yes," he said.

"I doubt it," she said.

"Well, I'll tell you one thing: If you keep 'em off when it's cold, you won't have no trouble keeping 'em off when it gets hot," he said.

In Montgomery the majority of bus riders were black, partic- ularly black women who went across town, from a world of black poverty to white affluence, to work as domestics. Never- theless, a black challenge to the bus company was a formidable undertaking. Despite the earlier ruling of the Supreme Court, the deep South remained totally segregated. Whites held complete political, judicial, and psychological power. In a city like Mont- gomery it was as if the Court had not ruled on *Brown*.

Racism Rampant in Montgomery

Before the whites would take the blacks seriously, the blacks had to take themselves seriously—that was the task facing the black leadership of Montgomery in December 1955. . . .

For many blacks, the bus line symbolized their powerlessness: Men were powerless to protect their wives and mothers from its indignities; women were powerless to protect their children. The Montgomery bus system, with its flexible segregation line, vested all authority in the bus driver himself, which, depending on his personality and mood, allowed humiliation to be heaped upon hu- miliation. There were, for instance, bus drivers who took a black customer's money and then, while the customer was walking around to enter through the back door, would roar off. . . .

A few months before Rosa Parks made her stand, a fifteen- year-old black girl had refused to give up her seat to a white and had been dragged from the bus ("She insisted she was colored and just as good as white," T.J. Ward, the arresting policeman, had noted with some surprise during the local court proceedings on her arrest). She had been charged with assault and battery for re- sisting arrest. For a time the black leadership thought of making hers the constitutional test case it sought, but backed off when someone learned that she was pregnant. So when Rosa Parks was arrested, the obvious response was a boycott. This was the blacks' strongest lever: They were the biggest group of riders, and with- out them it was not going to be a very profitable bus service.

The Movement Gains a Great Leader

One of their great problems was the terrible divisions within the black leadership itself—by religion, by generation, by age, by class. There was no doubt that Ed Nixon was a forceful figure, willing on many occasions to take risks that few others would; but some felt that he was too abrasive, too eager for glory, and not sensitive enough to others. At the first organizational meeting, held the day after Parks was arrested, there was quick agreement on the need for a one-day boycott, starting on Monday morning. There was also a decision to hold a meeting of the black leadership, which included many ministers, on Monday afternoon, and a large public protest meeting was set for Monday night. . . . Before the [afternoon] meeting was over, Martin Luther King, Jr., was named president of the new group, to be called the Montgomery Improvement Association (MIA). It was not a role he sought, but he was the obvious choice—in no small part because he was relatively new on the scene and belonged to no faction of the city's black leadership. There were other reasons as well: His congregation was unusually affluent and therefore less vulnerable to white reprisals. Finally, a number of people did not want Nixon to be the leader, yet King got on relatively well with Nixon, who had heard King speak earlier that year at an NAACP meeting and had been impressed. "I don't know how I'm going to do it," Nixon told a friend of his who taught at Alabama State, "but someday I'm going to hitch him to the stars." King himself did not necessarily want to be hitched to the stars; he was wary of taking on too much responsibility and had only recently turned down an offer to head the local NAACP. After all, he was new in town, had a young family, and wanted first and foremost to do a good job at his first church.

But with a certain inevitability the movement sought him. He was a brilliant speaker. He had the ability to make complex ideas simple: By repeating phrases, he could expand an idea, blending the rational with the emotional. That gave him the great ability to move others, blacks at first and soon, remarkably enough, whites as well. He could reach people of all classes and backgrounds; he could inspire men and women with nothing but his words. . . .

That night, most of the black people of Montgomery got their first taste of Martin King's oratory. He started out by making one point clear: Their boycott was different from those of the White Citizens' Councils, which were using the threat of violence to stop black political and legal progress in the deep South. "Now, let us say that we are not here advocating violence. We have overcome that. I want it to be known throughout Montgomery and throughout the nation that we are a Christian people. The only weapon that we have in our hands this evening is the weapon of protest." They were nothing less than ordinary

Americans, he was saying, seeking the most ordinary of American rights in a democracy they loved as much as white people loved it. They were, in effect, setting out to make America whole. "If we are wrong, the Constitution of the United States is wrong. If we are wrong, God Almighty is wrong. If we are wrong, Jesus of Nazareth was merely a utopian dreamer and never came down to earth! If we are wrong, justice is a lie." By then the crowd was with him, cheering each incantation. "And we are determined here in Montgomery to work and fight until justice runs down like water and righteousness like a mighty stream." When it was over, it was clear that the right man had arrived in the right city at the right time; this would be no one-day boycott but one that would continue until the white community addressed black grievances. . . .

When the bus boycott began, Martin Luther King, Jr., was twenty-six years old; he had been in Montgomery only fifteen months. He was a black Baptist Brahmin, a symbol of the new, more confident, better educated black leaders now just beginning to appear in the postwar South. . . .

To the white leadership in Montgomery, Martin King was just another faceless preacher, surely ignorant. The popular caricature of a black minister was of a whooper and hollerer. Indeed, the whites kept calling him Preacher King at the beginning of the boycott, as if by denying him his proper title they could diminish him. He fought against such stereotyping with careful formality. . . .

White Leaders Struggle to End the Boycott

The white community had no idea how to deal with the boycott. The city leadership thought it was dealing with the black leadership from the past—poorly educated, readily divided, lacking endurance, and without access to national publicity outlets. When the boycott proved to be remarkably successful on the first day, the mayor of Montgomery, W.A. Gayle, did not sense that something historic was taking place, nor did he move to accommodate the blacks, who were in fact not asking for integrated buses but merely a minimal level of courtesy and a fixed line between the sections. Gayle turned to a friend and said, "Comes the first rainy day and the Negroes will be back on the buses." Soon it did rain, but the boycott continued. As the movement grew stronger, the principal response of Gayle and his two commissioners was to join the White Citizens' Council. A month after the boycott began, it proved so successful that the bus-line operators were asking for permission to double the price from ten to twenty cents a ride. They were granted a five-cent raise. In late January, frustrated by the solidarity of the blacks, the white leadership went to three relatively obscure black ministers and tricked them into saying, or at least seeming to say, that they accepted the city's terms and would show up at a meeting at city hall. Then the *Montgomery Advertiser* was brought in—a disgraceful moment for a newspaper—to report on the alleged agreement and make it seem, without using the names of the three ministers, that the real black leadership had conceded. By chance the real black leadership found out, and the ploy was not successful. But it was a sign of how terrified and out of touch the white leadership was—as if it could, by means of disinformation, halt a movement as powerful as this. When the hoax was discovered, the mayor was petulant. No more Mr. Nice Guy, he threatened. "No other city in the South of our size has treated the Negroes more fairly," he said. Now he wanted his fellow whites to be made of sterner stuff and to stop helping their maids and workers to get to work by giving them transportation money and worse, giving them rides. . . .

Inevitably, the city leaders resorted to what had always worked in the past: the use of police power. The city fathers decided that it had to break the back of the carpool, and soon the police started arresting carpool drivers. On January 26, 1956, some eight weeks into the boycott, Martin Luther King, Jr., was arrested for driving 30 miles an hour in a 25-mile-an-hour zone. He was taken to the police station and fingerprinted; at first it appeared that he would be kept overnight, but because the crowd of blacks outside the station kept growing larger and noisier, the police let King go on his own recognizance. Two days later, King's house was bombed by a white extremist, the first in a series of such incidents at the homes of black leaders and at black churches.

The Boycott Attracts National Attention

In unity and nonviolence the blacks found new strength, particularly as the nation began to take notice. Things that had for so long terrified them—the idea of being arrested and spending the night in prison, for example—became a badge of honor. Their purpose now was greater than their terror. More, because the nation was watching, the jails were becoming safer. King was, in effect, taking a crash course in the uses of modern media and proving a fast learner. Montgomery was becoming a big story, and the longer it went on, the bigger it became. In the past it had been within the power of such papers as the *Advertiser* and its afternoon twin, the far more racist *Alabama Journal,* either to grant or not grant coverage to black protests and to slant the coverage in terms most satisfying to the whites. The power to deny coverage was a particularly important aspect of white authority, for if coverage was denied, the blacks would feel isolated and gradually lose heart (for taking such risks without anyone knowing or caring); in addition, the whites would be able to crush any protest with far fewer witnesses and far less scrutiny. But that power deserted the local newspapers now, in no small part because the Montgomery story was too important for even the most virulently segregationist newspaper to ignore completely, affecting as it did virtually every home in the city; second, because even when the local newspapers tried to control the coverage, and at the very least minimize it, the arrival of television meant that the newspapers were no longer the only potential journalistic witnesses. . . .

Like many of his generation, [a young TV reporter named Frank McGee] was aware that he was riding a very good story. That was particularly true as the whites blindly continued to resist and the story continued to escalate. The NBC network news show, also still in its infancy, started to use McGee with increasing regularity on the network, with a direct feed from Montgomery. It was not only a good story, in which ordinary Americans were asserting their demands for the most basic rights, but it was also helping McGee's career, which for a young, toughminded, ambitious reporter was almost an unbeatable combination. (Within a year of the bus settlement, Frank McGee became one of NBC's first national network correspondents.) Events were soon beyond the ability of the *Advertiser* to control coverage. Montgomery was soon flooded with members of the national press, causing [the paper's editor] Grover Hall to comment that he was "duenna and Indian guide to more than a hundred reporters of the international press." The more coverage there was, the more witnesses there were and the harder it was for the white leadership to inflict physical violence upon the blacks. In addition, the more coverage there was, the more it gave courage to the leadership and its followers. The sacrifices and the risks were worth it, everyone sensed, because the country and the world were now taking notice. What was at stake in the *Advertiser*'s coverage of Martin King and the Montgomery bus boycott was, the editors of that paper soon learned to their surprise, not King's reputation but the *Advertiser*'s reputation. . . .

The Supreme Court Declares Bus Segregation Unconstitutional

On November 13, 1956, almost a year after the boycott had begun, King went to court to defend himself and the carpools against the local authorities who had declared it "a public nuisance." King was hardly optimistic about the outcome in a Montgomery court, but suddenly, during a recess, an AP reporter handed him a note that included an AP bulletin reporting that the Supreme Court had judged the Montgomery bus-segregation law to be unconstitutional. The blacks had won. King, always aware of the need to include rather than exclude people and the need to be magnanimous in victory, spoke at a mass rally to point out this should not be viewed as victory of blacks over whites but as a victory for American justice and democracy. On December 21, the city prepared to desegregate its buses. An empty bus pulled up to a corner near Dr. King's home. Martin Luther King, Jr., boarded it. The white driver smiled at him and said, "I believe you are Reverend King." "Yes, I am," Martin Luther King, Jr., said. "We are glad to have you with us this morning," the driver said.

So the battle was won. But the war was hardly over. It was a beginning rather than an end; the boycott became the Movement, with a capital *M*. The blacks might have alienated the local white leadership, but they had gained the sympathy of the white majority outside the South. In the past the whites in Montgomery had been both judge and jury: Now, as the nation responded to the events there, they became the judged.

Elvis "the King of Rock and Roll" Presley
Signs with RCA: December 1955

Elvis as a Catalyst for Change in Popular Music

by Patsy Guy Hammontree

When RCA chose Elvis Presley as its ticket into the rising rock-and-roll movement, it could not have imagined the impact that Presley would have on both the company and popular music. Once RCA began producing Presley's records and releasing them, the company knew it had a winner. Presley was soon topping the charts with his songs and making appearances on popular shows such as *The Ed Sullivan Show.* His career skyrocketed until he went into the army in March 1958, where he served until 1960. During that time he released only one record. When he resumed his career he was successful, but he never quite regained the popularity he enjoyed during the late 1950s. During the 1970s he steadily declined due to physical problems and drug addictions. His death in 1977 from a drug overdose was a reminder of the excesses of rock and roll.

Despite Presley's decline over the years, he is still the reigning "King of Rock and Roll." His influence on his contemporaries and on future generations of musicians is immense. He also changed the culture of the 1950s, challenging conformity in race relations, sexuality, and musical styles. He managed to forge black and white music into a style that was palatable to the mainstream. At the same time, he represented much of what Americans had always loved about their culture. His roots were in blues, gospel, and bluegrass, and his story was a classic rags-to-riches tale.

Beyond the 1950s, Presley influenced a wide range of musicians, many of whom were prominent in their own right. The Beatles, for example, credited Presley along with other early American rock-and-roll musicians with inspiring their music. Today Presley's legacy is alive through his music and his status as a major cultural icon.

Patsy Guy Hammontree is an award-winning professor of English at the University of Tennessee who has a special interest in popular culture. In addition to *Elvis Presley: A Bio-Bibliography*, she is the author of *Shirley Temple Black: A Bio-Bibliography* and a contributor to *The Greenwood Guide to American Popular Culture*.

I t is curious to speculate just how history will treat Elvis Presley. Elvis's impact is a result of his passion for perfection as an entertainer, his vulnerability, his self-deprecating humor, and perhaps most of all, his kindness to fans; but those nebulous facets may not get recorded in the Presley chronicle. When the people who were so much affected by him are no longer alive to speak to the strength of his personality, the essence of Elvis may be lost. It is impossible to know if the existing evidence—three television specials along with the two documentaries—will be sufficient to exemplify his extraordinary impact as a personality. Written accounts often fail to give a good sense of his effect on audiences; therefore, if visual mediums fail, history will more than likely evaluate him solely as a singer. Indeed, he can stand as a singer, but social and cultural historians should not overlook his being much more. Elvis himself never publicly claimed to be a cultural force. For instance, at the 1958 dockside press conference when he shipped out for Germany, Elvis remarked, "I've been very lucky. I happened to come along at a time in the music business when there was no trend. I was lucky. The people were looking for something different, and I was lucky. I came along just in time." This unassuming remark reveals Elvis's perception of himself as an accident of history. The lure of egocentricity was tempered by his sincere belief that a mysterious metaphysical power made his status possible.

Merging Musical Styles for Mainstream Listeners

Whatever he privately thought about his personal success, he was right in noting that in 1955 there was no musical trend. The last major shift in music came in the twenties when jazz made its way into the musical mainstream. Black musicians had been playing jazz since before the turn of the century, and gradually white musicians became attracted to it. Ironically, in the mid-fifties, black music again affected a change in music. This time, Elvis Presley was the major transmitter. Rhythm and blues, which was so much a part of black musical heritage, moved into the white musical arena. For years, rhythm and blues was labeled "race music." According to some music scholars, however, black music is the only true American folk music; but "hillbilly" music of Appalachia is also American folk music. Either form is more authentic than the stylized "folk" music of the sixties. Unfortunately for many people folk music has no other meaning. That is why it has been difficult for the general listener to recognize that Elvis Presley's "rockabilly" singing in the mid-fifties was a fusing of two folk music traditions. Bringing new life to popular music, he changed its direction forever.

From the twenties to the fifties, most American music was standardized and predictable. World War II, of course, had an effect on music. Patriotic songs were much in demand from 1940 through 1945, but on the whole popular music was romantic and sentimental, as might be expected during a time of national trauma. Almost as an antidote were novelty songs such as "Marzie Doats and Dozy Doats and Little Lambs Eat Ivy," "Flat Foot Floozie with a Floy, Floy," and "Hut Sut Song on the Rillah Rah"; these songs were short lived, and they created no trend. Pop music consisted essentially same type of Tinpan Alley tunes popular since the twenties, clichéd both instrumentally and lyrically. As music scholar Sidney Finkelstein put it, "Music had straight-jacket forms and censored inane words." Then hard on the heels of World War II came the Korean War, again placing together servicemen from different regions, engendering cultural development, and affecting musical trends.

The two wars contributed to Elvis Presley's success. From the beginning of World War II in 1941 to the end of the Korean "conflict" in 1953, much of the American population was on the move. Traditionally, this country has a mobile population, but during this twelve-year period, movement was extensive. World War II made jobs at defense plants plentiful, but plants were not equally distributed in all regions. To get jobs, people had to move, particularly Southerners, since almost no heavy industry existed anywhere in the Southeast. Naturally, people took regional cultural patterns with them, gradually integrating what they brought with what was there when they arrived. Military assignments also contributed to change. Young men were stationed in parts of the country and parts of the world they would otherwise never have visited, and they took their musical preferences with them. Further, USO entertainment, designed to satisfy troops from all parts of the country, provided programs with mixed musical genres. Thus, this relocation of people set in motion significant cultural changes, one being the alteration of musical tastes.

The Emergence of Two American Musical Styles

As regional cultures intermingled, two distinctly regional types of music, both of which had been generally viewed as lacking in musical style and grace, began to reach the ears of a wider audience. Hillbilly music (now identified as country and western) and "race" music (now identified as rhythm and blues), took on new importance despite their neglect by musical aficionados. As Sidney Finkelstein points out in *How Music Expresses Ideas,* persons influential in dictating musical tastes considered only established European compositions worthy of attention. In Finkelstein's words, "Concert music and opera were predominantly a luxury imported from Europe, patronized by the rich as a plaything in imitation of the European aristocracy, and kept largely for the rich." Other music was considered uncouth. "Pop" music was tolerated; it was, after all, the music of the masses. Jazz had status among certain small elite groups, but rhythm and blues remained unnoticed. Southern mountain music was, on the whole, viewed as quaint but not musically important. The Appalachian poor provided themselves with music since most families had a guitar. Those who could afford radios tuned in to hillbilly stations. Most Southern towns which had stations played plenty of hillbilly music, and there was always Nashville's WSM, a clear channel 50,000 watt station which has broadcast the "Grand Ole Opry" since 1925. Blacks in urban areas—if the city were large enough—could hear their music on stations catering to black audiences. In predominantly rural areas if there was not a city large enough to support a black station, blacks, like Appalachian whites, made their own music, providing the rhythm and blues reservoirs from which ultimately came mainstream rock and roll.

Black music, as have other black art forms, has moved slowly into the cultural mainstream. Country music gained national recognition more quickly because it reached a wider audience. Black music reached its audience largely through mail order record companies which exploited the rural Southern market but had no interest in the music or the musicians. Such cavalier attitudes on the part of people processing and distributing the records further hampered the assimilation of black artists into the larger culture. As late as 1950 most white Americans were ignorant of the black sound, their awareness limited to Negro spirituals. Some persons were cognizant of the black origins of jazz and "blues"; rhythm music, however, was essentially a foreign sound to white audiences, and the possibility of its becoming more familiar was greatly limited. Hillbilly music, on the other hand, did have the "Grand Ole Opry," which went out over the powerful WSM, widely disseminating the Appalachian sound. Radio owners and programmers assumed that white Americans did not enjoy black music and advertisers were not eager to sponsor it. Black music was heard primarily on Sundays. Stations often sold or donated time to black church services; but not many whites heard those programs since they were aired in the non-peak time slots.

Further, blacks had no recording studios in the South, their nearest outlet being Chicago. Occasionally Chicago-based organizations would transport equipment to the South, Memphis in particular, for limited recording sessions. In the early fifties, an entrepreneur named Sam Phillips organized Sun Records and the Memphis Recording Studio upon seeing the business possibilities in establishing a local recording station for blacks. Ironically, black music recorded at Phillips's studio was not released on the Sun label; it was pressed on other labels.

Black Music Is Promoted to White Listeners

Much later, Phillips took on legendary status as the man who gave Elvis Presley a chance. Allegedly he wanted to find a white singer who could duplicate the sound of black music, making it palatable to white audiences. His story has become highly romanticized. Supposedly Phillips grew up hearing black music at the knee of a black man who worked for his family in Alabama, and he became attached to black music. Indeed, he no doubt heard much black music, but business more than sentiment was the motivating factor in Phillips's decision to open a recording studio for black artists.

Meantime, a late-night WSM program sponsored by Randy's Record Shop in Gallatin, Tennessee, played some of the first rhythm and blues on traditional white radio. For the early fifties, the program had a liberal sprinkling of "race music." Gradually, the rhythm songs of blacks began to creep into white pop music. Helping the progression was the film *Blackboard Jungle,* released in 1955. Set in a ghetto of New York City, it depicted conflict between a humane white teacher and a group of black and Hispanic students who were suspicious of all whites. The movie soundtrack featured Bill Haley and the Comets, a group of musicians in their late thirties or early forties who had begun to include rhythm and blues numbers in their club acts. One of the film's dominant musical numbers was "Shake, Rattle and Roll," a song already well known to black audiences. As movie background music, it reached the ears of many Americans who never would have heard music either from Randy's Record Shop or from any predominantly black radio station. The rhythmic beat of the song caught on, and it provided an extraordinary boost for black music.

The Youth Market Opens Up

Further, in the mid-fifties, a technological advance facilitated the spread of music in ways not previously possible. Prior to that time, record players were expensive apparatuses. They were often built into a radio console, making them even more costly. The prohibitive price kept them out of range for the average wage earner with a limited amount to spend on entertainment. RCA, in an innovative move, began manufacturing a small record player suited to the new 45 r.p.m. records. Not only was this new record player priced inexpensively, it could also play up to six records at one time, having an automatic device to drop the records. Both the inexpensive records and the reasonably priced record players were now within reach of many who had never before considered the possibility of owning what was essentially a personal phonograph. Young people for the first time could have an influence on the popularity of records.

Elvis Ushers in Rock and Roll

The confluence of these factors meant a musical watershed was inevitable. The highly unlikely figure who emerged to have a phenomenal effect not only on music but also other cultural aspects was an unknown—Elvis Presley. With his peculiar style of dress and shrill singing voice (a combination of the falsetto singing of black artists and the whining singing of hillbillies), this young white man with long sideburns and a large, heavily greased pompadour merged the two strains of American folk music—Negro and Appalachian—and gave it a hybrid existence. Elvis was then actually swept along by the swift movement of musical changes. As Glenn Hardin, Elvis's long-time pianist, remarked,

> Elvis was definitely one of the innovators of our time. The music he recorded to start with—that was all wrong to try to start with. People trying to break into the business begin with music that's already accepted and familiar. He didn't do that. He came out with music that was really a new sound to most people. Helping him of course was the fact that he had an exceptional voice that was different from anybody else's. It's a very good voice. It makes a song distinct. I think the turning in music, it would have happened. I don't know when or who would have done it. But it would have happened because music changes every so often. But I don't think it would have been *that* big. There was something about Elvis that made a big—that had a big effect. They'd write after each record, "He's a flash in the pan. He'll never make it." But Elvis had talent. If he hadn't had talent, he couldn't have lasted. People figure it out after a while when a person doesn't have talent. These things don't happen very often. Elvis wasn't exactly first, but he was there when things began to stir a little bit. And he was good.

It is true that Elvis did not single-handedly initiate the movement to a new kind of music, but he did more than any other white musician of the time to advance it. Moreover, in addition to his voice, which attracted many people to him, he had a personal appeal which made his influence stretch beyond his own immediate popularity. He became a cultural curiosity without ever intending to be anything more than a popular singer who had ambitions to someday be an actor.

12 The Soviets Launch *Sputnik*: October 4, 1957

Sputnik Had Far-Reaching Consequences

by Alan J. Levine

In 1957 most Americans were content and relatively secure. The Cold War did not intrude on daily life in a prominent way. Americans felt good about their country, perceiving it as a nation that was strong, financially secure, and progressive.

This confident sense of security was shaken, however, on October 4, 1957, when the Russians announced their successful launch of *Sputnik*, an artificial satellite designed to orbit the earth. This news startled the United States because Americans believed they were technologically superior to the Soviet Union. After all, America was the land of great inventors like Thomas Edison, Robert Fulton, and Henry Ford. Further, the capitalist system encouraged and rewarded innovation. It was part of the American culture and identity, so the Russians surpassing them in the field of space technology was unsettling.

The implications were frightening. Americans worried that the Russians would put a man in space first. There was a joke that asked, "What will Americans find on the other side of the moon?" The punch line was "Russians." Another, more pressing concern was that space weapons—both defensive and offensive—would be next. The Cold War took on a new and troubling demeanor. To make matters worse, President Dwight D. Eisenhower seemed unconcerned. He downplayed *Sputnik*, claiming it meant nothing.

What the public did not know, but Eisenhower did, was that

American researchers were making significant advances. Eisenhower had given each military branch a set of goals and a budget to achieve them, and they were well on their way to reaching them. Although the Americans fell behind temporarily during the late 1950s, they proved their technological superiority in the long run.

Alan J. Levine is an author and historian with expertise in Russian history, World War II, the Cold War, and international affairs. He has written numerous articles and books, including *The Soviet Union, the Communist Movement, and the World: Prelude to the Cold War* (1992) and *The War Against Rommel's Supply Lines, 1942–1943* (1999).

D espite ample warnings, on October 4, 1957 Americans were startled to learn that the Soviets had put Sputnik I, a 2-foot sphere weighing 184 pounds, into orbit. (*Sputnik* means "fellow-traveler." Russian astronomers had long used this term to describe hypothetical small natural satellites of the earth.) Sputnik I had little scientific instrumentation, but it carried two radio transmitters that emitted a beep that Americans found maddening. It was far larger than the Vanguard satellite and had to have been launched by an ICBM [intercontinental ballistic missile]. On November 3, the Soviets launched the much bigger and heavily instrumented Sputnik II, which weighed 1,120 pounds and carried a dog. (Wits called it "Muttnik.") Moreover, Sputnik II remained attached to the R-7's empty sustainer; over 8,000 pounds had gone into orbit. Some thought Sputnik II had been launched by a new rocket, perhaps using some sort of superfuel, or even a nuclear rocket.

The Implications of the New "Space Age"

What was known about Sputnik I seemed bad enough. The fact that the Soviets had an ICBM, and a big one, when the United States had yet to test successfully the far smaller Atlas, finally sank in. (That the Soviet ICBM was too big was hardly suspected at the time.) And the Soviets, not the West, had the glory of launching what was immediately called the Space Age. This was a vast gain in prestige for the Communist powers and a terrific morale blow to the West. Furthermore, it seemed to imply two related but different dangers that were often confused in the 1950s.

First, if the Soviet ICBM was reliable and effective and put into mass production, and if the Americans failed to catch up or take vital counteractions, the Soviets might gain a first-strike capability within a few years.

If they turned their undoubted lead in development into a massive superior ICBM force, the West's development lag would turn into what became known as a "missile gap." And this might become an actual "deterrent gap," a situation in which the Soviets could attack without fear of effective retaliation. The distinction between a missile gap and a deterrent gap must be stressed, for the Eisenhower Administration had expected a missile gap for a while but was fairly sure that it could prevent a deterrent gap. (It must also be stressed that the missile gap was a forecast or prediction, *not* a statement about the current balance of power.) The Administration expected to prevent the expected Soviet superiority in numbers from becoming an effective first-strike capability.

The second problem might be called a space or payload gap. The R-7 (not to mention anything bigger that the Soviets might build) ensured that, at least for some years, the Soviets could send bigger loads into space than the Americans, score any number of firsts, and exploit any military advantage that might be found in space. As it turned out, the R-7's defects, among other things, prevented a missile gap. But the space gap was real. The United States matched the Soviet ability to lift heavy loads into space only in 1963. But its superiority in electronic miniaturization and the large number of satellites it launched meant that, in practice, it achieved more than the Soviets in terms of scientific results and utilization of outer space.

Sputnik Shakes American Confidence

Sputnik triggered a political and even social explosion in the West. Even when it was understood, as it was in the United States (but *not* in Europe), that there was no immediate military danger and that the West would retain military superiority at least for the near future, there was a great disillusionment. Many had been sure that the West, and especially the United States, would always have technological superiority and that this would compensate for the (rather exaggerated) numerical superiority of the Communist powers and the political initiative the latter held in the Cold War. Apart from what now seems a touching faith that the United States would always lead the world technologically, most Westerners had assumed that the West must be ahead simply because it was a free society. That state of mind had already survived much contrary evidence—notably the excellence of most Soviet equipment and the actual superiority of their tanks during World War II; their unexpectedly early achievement of nuclear weapons; and the trouble the Mig-15 had given Western pilots in Korea. But the fact that a totalitarian state had led the way into space could not be effaced; and even after it was clear that the West was ahead in military missiles, the Soviets would score spectacular firsts. There were fears that the Soviets might spring almost any kind of surprise; not just bigger and better missiles and satellites, but rocket bombers and nuclear-powered rockets and planes.

There was no counterpart to this general anxiety before or after. The Air Force and some congressional critics had feared a "bomber gap" in 1955–1956, wrongly thinking that the Soviets were building more heavy bombers than the United States. However, that short-lived worry had only a mild effect on defense policy, and there is little evidence that the public was much perturbed. Later anxieties, during the 1970s and 1980s, focused on comparatively narrow issues of Soviet superiority in this or that particular item, possibly gained only by violating arms-control agreements—not a general fear that the Soviets were indeed the wave of the future and about to overtake the West on a broad front. The fears of the late 1950s were thus unique.

For a time, those fears were real and powerful. The *London Times* spoke of a world transformed, in political and psychological terms, by Sputnik. The general belief, rarely questioned at the time, that the West faced a technologically superior enemy that might soon enjoy outright superiority makes that era one of the most interesting (and perhaps most misunderstood) periods of the Cold War. (Contrary to what is often claimed, such overestimation of the other side was not common during the Cold War.). . .

The Post-Sputnik Furor

Late 1957 might not have been a particularly pleasant time in any case. The United States was in its worst recession since the 1930s, and the President had suffered his second serious illness; this worried even (or perhaps especially) those who did not admire him. Since the Suez crisis and the Hungarian Revolution, international tension had been growing.

After Sputnik, bad luck and blunders by the Administration's officials and defenders made its position worse. The post-Sputnik controversy is arguably a study in how not to handle an issue. Critics pointed to ill-considered official reactions, some by individuals with no responsibility for defense matters, and played up contradictions and misstatements, while the Administration was forced, over the course of a month, to concede that things were worse than it had first admitted.

On October 8, the President declared that there was no space race and that Sputnik had not raised his apprehensions one iota, although he sportingly conceded that it was a great achievement. Yet his first television address in response to Sputnik contained seeming evasions and one or two poorly worded passages that wrongly suggested that he was ill-informed about missiles. Secretary [of Defense Charles] Wilson denied, on October 9, that he had ordered any sort of speedup of the missile program, although he was doing just that, and he insisted that the satellite had no military impact and that the Soviets currently had no operational ICBMs. While those points were perfectly correct, Wilson's offhand manner made a bad impression. Critics quickly unearthed his November 1954 remark that he did not care if the Soviets got a satellite first. Others offered more recent unfortunate remarks. Eisenhower's chief of staff, Sherman Adams, declared that the Administration was not interested in an "outer space basketball game"; he later conceded that to be an "overemphasis on the deemphasis." Clarence Randall, an Eisenhower assistant on economic matters, described Sputnik as a "silly bauble." Admiral Rawson Bennett, head of naval research, derided Sputnik as a "hunk of iron almost anybody could launch." Although that remark was designed to boost the morale of the Vanguard team, it contributed to the impression that the Administration was asleep. Administration spokespeople blunderingly tried to counter critics by inflating expenditures on research and development, reclassifying expenses more properly charged to procurement and production and even housekeeping at research facilities. Some fanatic partisans even suggested that Sputnik was somehow a fake. Many whined that Sputnik was due to the fact that the Soviets had grabbed the Germans responsible for developing the V-2. Even the usually careful Secretary of State, John Foster Dulles, at first gave credence to that absurdity, which was quickly exposed and rebounded against the Administration. Vigorous efforts by Eisenhower, Dulles, and the Vice President never effaced the impression that the Administration was unaware of what was at stake. Dulles, taking a line that he stuck to later, suggested that Sputnik might be a good thing, preventing complacency in the West. A real military danger, he noted, was five or ten years off.

Criticism of the Administration

The Administration's critics neatly made their case, which was crystallized by the remark of the most respected American labor leader, Walter Reuther, that Sputnik was a "bloodless Pearl Harbor." However exaggerated that seemed later, the spirit of the Americans of the 1950s was summarized by Reuther's promise that workers would make any sacrifice needed to catch up.

Those with specialized knowledge of missile matters, who had argued for speeding up the ICBM effort before Sputnik, were vocal. Senator Stuart Symington declared, "If this now known Soviet superiority develops into supremacy, the position of the Free World will be critical." Henry Jackson bluntly declared that "we are losing" the race for the ICBM. *Aviation Week* and *Missiles and Rockets,* long critical of the Administration, saw their version of events become gospel. Former Administration officials were powerful witnesses for the prosecution. Gardner's attacks on Secretary Wilson (but not the credit he gave the Administration for reviving the ICBM) were widely cited. Clifford Furnas, former Assistant Secretary of Defense for Research and Development, eloquently blamed Wilson for rejecting repeated requests for more money for research. Wilson, not much liked in or outside the Administration, was a particularly good target; he seemed the very caricature of a Republican big businessman. General Maxwell Taylor, recently retired as Army Chief of Staff, blamed interservice rivalry for the missile lag. The *New York Times* warned in November 1957 that the United States was in a race for survival. It reported [American engineer Wehner] von Braun's estimate that the United States was five years behind the Soviets. Even Republican politicians and institutions turned against the Administration; the Luce publications printed indictment after indictment of its real and alleged mistakes, culminating in an incredible article in the November 18 *Life,* accurately titled "Arguing the Case for Being Panicky.". . .

The generally conservative ethos of the Eisenhower Administration (indeed of the entire period since 1945), which was oriented toward business and private initiative, was discredited. There was a renewal of faith in an enlarged government role in economics and society, in planning, and in what was optimistically called social engineering (social alchemy would have been a more accurate term). Sputnik and the apparent general advance of the U.S.S.R. seemed to validate, if not socialism or nationalization, a more positive role for government. After all, the Soviets seemed to be succeeding and even surpassing the capitalist world. Such ideas influenced many with no sympathy at all for Communism or even democratic socialism. They fused with, and furthered, the pretensions of the social scientists of the era. It would be foolish to attribute the growth of liberal or leftist ideas solely to the shock of Sputnik; however, Sputnik played a serious role in discrediting the existing order, which seemed to have failed in its own terms.

European Attitudes

Europeans reacted far more strongly than people in North America to Sputnik. Whatever its other misfortunes, the Eisenhower Administration quickly reassured Americans that the United States was still stronger than the Soviets and that any real danger was still some way off. In Europe, things were different. A week after Sputnik I, a Dutch delegate to the Western European Union attacked the United States for having "helped our enemy" by not getting an ICBM first. The European NATO [North Atlantic Treaty Organization] members became extremely skittish about allowing IRBM [intermediate range ballistic missile] bases in their countries. There was a general belief (except in Italy), which persisted until 1961, that the Soviets had already overtaken the Americans technologically and in military strength. There was a corresponding tendency of Europeans to distance themselves from the United States. However, this was not the case among the British, who reacted to the perceived threat by becoming more pro-American. Still, while continental Europeans' attitudes changed, they did not bolt the alliance. NATO was not quite as weak as alarmists periodically suggested; although there was a good deal of trouble, resistance to the Soviets did not crumble. . . .

America Attempts to Launch Its Own Satellite

Despite the Administration's increasingly vigorous actions, the nation and the West were demoralized further on December 6, 1957 by the failure of the first Vanguard satellite.

Shortly after Sputnik, Dr. John P. Hagen personally briefed the President about the next Vanguard firing. Vanguard TV-3 would carry a "minimal satellite" weighing just 4 pounds, but it was primarily the first test of the whole launch vehicle. Hagen warned that success was not guaranteed; in fact a successful satellite would be a bonus. He would have preferred that the launch get no publicity beforehand. But on October 9, the President's press secretary issued a statement which, while technically accurate, lent itself to the interpretation that a successful satellite was expected.

On December 6, TV-3 rose a few feet; then its engine cut off, and it fell back and collapsed in a spectacular burst of flame. If only because of the atmosphere surrounding the episode, it was a sight that none who saw was likely to forget. The exact cause was never resolved precisely, although there was a bitter feud between the contractors. The engine was slightly modified and never failed in the same way again.

But that was small consolation to the public, which was influenced by a press that reacted to the exaggerated expectations it had fostered. TV-3 became not an ordinary failure of an experimental rocket, but a symbol and a national humiliation. Dubbed "Flopnik" or "Kaputnik," it was played up throughout the world. The Americans, it seemed, could not even orbit a mere grapefruit. Those working on Vanguard were treated like lepers; even the successful Atlas test on December 17, militarily far more important than Vanguard, failed to cut through the gloom.

Final Success with Explorer

A real defeatist neurosis was developing. It could have gotten out of hand easily, for the next Vanguard firing, in February, would also fail. Fortunately for the West, the Eisenhower Administration finally used the Army's satellite capability.

The incoming Secretary of Defense, Neil McElroy, happened to be at Huntsville when Sputnik I went up. Von Braun and Medaris promised to orbit a satellite in ninety days if allowed to do so. On October 8, in one of his first policy shifts after Sputnik, Eisenhower ordered the outgoing Wilson to let the Army prepare as a backup. Medaris, on his own, had von Braun demothball a Jupiter C and start work. On November 8, it was officially announced that the Army would launch a satellite as part of the IGY [International Geophysical Year, the time from July

1957 to December, 1958 dedicated to scientific advancement around the globe and in near-earth space], but the directive that reached Medaris told him only to prepare to do so. Angry, Medaris threatened to resign before receiving an unambiguous authorization.

The Jet Propulsion Laboratory repackaged instruments from Vanguard. Equipment designed for the spherical Vanguard satellite had to be altered to fit into the long, thin Explorer, which used conventional batteries instead of the solar cells used by Vanguard. Explorer I carried two radios to report the temperature of its outer surface and interior, micrometeorite impacts, and the detection of cosmic rays. The cosmic-ray experiment had been designed by James Van Allen of the University of Iowa.

By late January 1958, the Jupiter C was ready. (Officially, it was the Juno I when carrying a live fourth stage and satellite, but in practice that name was hardly used.) Explorer I was launched on January 31; jetstream winds kicked it into a slightly higher orbit than planned. The satellite and the attached fourth stage together weighed just 30 pounds; but there was great jubilation and relief. Within a short time, Explorer I made the first great scientific discovery of the Space Age: the Van Allen radiation belts.

Explorer was a landmark in the space program. It was not just its first great success, but the first time that von Braun's group, which had been in the United States for over a decade, was used properly. The group had been underused or shunted to secondary tasks; only now did it move to the center of American rocket development—and for space exploration rather than military missiles.

America's Defense Is Bolstered

Explorer and ABMA [Army Ballistic Missile Agency] involvement in space were only the first, most visible examples of a general post-Sputnik shift in Administration policy during 1957–1958, which affected both military and space efforts. Contrary to what is sometimes claimed, Sputnik had a considerable impact on the conduct of American defense. Defense expenditures were increased. In January 1958, the Administration requested an additional $1.37 billion for defense, and in April it returned to Congress for another $1.45 billion. The late Eisenhower era military buildup did not equal that of the [Harry] Truman, [John F.] Kennedy, and, [Ronald] Reagan Administrations, but it was nev-

ertheless considerable. Its main peculiarity was that it was limited to strategic weapons; their share of the military budget peaked
in 1959, reaching a proportion never equaled before or after. . . .

The Long-Term Impact of Sputnik

The commotion after Sputnik showed the Americans of the
1950s at their best, but also at their worst. On the one hand, there
was an outpouring of real concern and energy and a determination to overtake the Soviets and cure the country's ills, much in
contrast to the bickering and languid response to decline char-
acteristic from the late 1960s onward. On the other hand, there
was a good deal of foolishness and profiteering, and a misuse of
patriotism by people with axes to grind, as well as ostrich-headed
reactions by those who pretended that the Soviet rockets did not
exist or that it was all because "we captured the wrong Germans." Some of the attacks on the Eisenhower Administration
were sheer lies.

John Foster Dulles had speculated, as early as October 16,
1957, that Sputnik would prove a good thing, a salutary shock
jolting Americans out of their complacency and reenergizing
American society. (This was a curious revelation in that even at
the top of the Administration some shared the prevailing ideas of
social criticism, at least in their conservative form.) Elaborating
on this three months later, Dulles suggested that Sputnik might
mark a decisive turn in the Cold War precisely because it would
boomerang by causing Americans to react.

Five or ten years later, in the high noon of the Kennedy-
[Lyndon B.] Johnson Administration, even many who disliked
Dulles would have conceded that he had proven farsighted. For
all the worry and trouble that had ensued in the three or four
years after Sputnik, it had galvanized the United States into taking a new look at its educational system and pouring more resources into science and technology as well as its missile and
space efforts. Militarily, the United States had maintained—even
increased—its lead over the U.S.S.R. Furthermore, the partisans
would argue, by embarrassing the staid incumbent it had helped
make possible the New Frontier and the Great Society. The late
1950s, it seemed, had been the start of a new burst of energy, activism, and readiness to make things over, all of which promised
a better society.

Decades later, the impact of Sputnik seems very different. The criticism of American society, which was fashionable in the late 1950s and afterward, contributed nothing to a better world, or less than nothing. The ranting against conformity and material- ism of the 1950s seems ludicrous. Except for racial discrimina- tion (in decline since at least the 1920s), none of the real social evils that such criticism had sometimes indicted were overcome; most became far worse, or indeed were exacerbated by new evils unthinkable in 1957. Appearances had not been entirely deceiv- ing in the late 1950s; there was a burst of energy and creativity. But most of it was misdirected; and what resulted was not the re- generation but the derailment of a society, which despite its faults had been progressing rapidly.

No more damning judgment can be imagined.

Sputnik Is Launched

by the New York Times

When the Soviet Union launched *Sputnik*, a 184-pound artificial satellite, on October 4, 1957, the space age was launched with it. Because of the Russian success with *Sputnik*, more attention and resources were dedicated to improving technology for American space exploration and machinery. The launch came toward the end of the International Geophysical Year, a period of research on the earth and global atmosphere by scientific communities worldwide. Both the United States and Russia declared their intentions to produce and launch satellites to collect scientific data.

During World War II, German researchers had made major advances in rocket technology. When Germany surrendered to the United States, many of these researchers immigrated to the United States and took their knowledge and expertise with them. While this was a boon to American space research, it took time to integrate the new researchers into the existing field. Further, American progress was held back by competition between military researchers and corporate researchers. Rather than share their findings and move more quickly toward groundbreaking technology, competing scientists kept their findings secret from one another. The Russians, however, began working on their space program immediately following the war and were more efficient thanks to cooperation instead of competition. Although bits of information about the Russians' progress were available, researchers in America largely ignored them. They still believed that American ingenuity and superior resources would outpace Russian efforts. They were wrong. As addled as they were by the launch of *Sputnik*, their concern heightened further when *Sputnik II* was launched twenty-nine days later, carrying a dog. This brought the Soviets even closer to the ultimate goal of putting people in space. The ability to launch spacecrafts carrying humans would greatly advance scientific knowledge and add a new dimension to defense and weapons possibilities. The Russians continued to put additional satellites into orbit, keeping the American sense of urgency alive. Finally, on January 31, 1958, the Americans successfully launched a thirty-one-pound satellite, *Explorer I*, into space.

The following article is taken from the story about *Sputnik* printed on the front page of the *New York Times*.

Moscow, Saturday, Oct. 5—The Soviet Union announced this morning that it successfully launched a man-made earth satellite into space yesterday.

The Russians calculated the satellite's orbit at a maximum at 560 miles above the earth and its speed at 18,000 miles an hour.

The official Soviet news agency Tass said the artificial moon, with a diameter of twenty-two inches and a weight of 184 pounds, was circling the earth once every hour and thirty-five minutes. This means more than fifteen times a day.

Two radio transmitters, Tass said, are sending signals continuously on frequencies of 20.005 and 40.002 megacycles. These signals were said to be strong enough to be picked up by amateur radio operators. The trajectory of the satellite is being tracked by numerous scientific stations.

Due over Moscow Today

Tass said the satellite was moving at an angle of 65 degrees to the equatorial plane and would pass over the Moscow area twice today.

"Its flight," the announcement added, "will be observed in the rays of the rising and setting sun with the aid of the simplest optical instruments, such as binoculars and spy-glasses."

The Soviet Union said the world's first satellite was "successfully launched" yesterday. Thus it asserted that it had put a scientific instrument into space before the United States. Washington has disclosed plans to launch a satellite next spring."

The Moscow announcement said the Soviet Union planned to send up more and bigger and heavier artificial satellites during the current International Geophysical Year, an eighteen-month period of study of the earth, its crust and the space surrounding it.

The rocket that carried the satellite into space left the earth at a rate of five miles a second, the Tass announcement said. Nothing was revealed, however, concerning the material of which the man-made moon was constructed or the site in the Soviet Union where the sphere was launched.

The Soviet Union said its sphere circling the earth had opened the way to inter-planetary travel.

It did not pass up the opportunity to use the launching for propaganda purposes. It said in its announcement that people now could see how "the new socialist society" had turned the boldest dreams of mankind into reality.

Moscow said the satellite was the result of years of study and research on the part of Soviet scientists.

Several Years of Study

Tass said:

"For several years the research and experimental designing work has been under way in the Soviet Union to create artificial satellites of the earth. It has already been reported in the press that the launching of the earth satellites in the U.S.S.R. had been planned in accordance with the program of International Geophysical Year research.

"As a result of intensive work by the research institutes and design bureaus, the first artificial earth satellite in the world has now been created. This first satellite was successfully launched in the U.S.S.R. October four."

The Soviet announcement said that as a result of the tremendous speed at which the satellite was moving it would burn up as soon as it reached the denser layers of the atmosphere. It gave no indication how soon that would be.

Military experts have said that the satellites would have no practicable military application in the foreseeable future. They said, however, that study of such satellites could provide valuable information that might be applied to flight studies for international ballistic missiles.

The satellites could not be used to drop atomic or hydrogen bombs or anything else on the earth, scientists have said. Nor could they be used in connection with the proposed plan for aerial inspection of military forces around the world.

An Aid to Scientists

Their real significance would be in providing scientists with important new information concerning the nature of the sun, cosmic radiation, solar radio interference and static-producing phenomena radiating from the north and south magnetic poles. All this information would be of inestimable value for those who are working on the problem of sending missiles and eventually men into the vast reaches of the solar system.

Publicly, Soviet scientists have approached the launching of the satellite with modesty and caution. On the advent of the International Geophysical Year last June they specifically disclaimed a desire to "race" the United States into the atmosphere with the little sphere.

The scientists spoke understandingly of "difficulties" they had heard described by their American counterparts. They refused several invitations to give any details about their own problems in designing the satellite and gave even less information than had been generally published about their work in the Soviet press.

Hinted at Launching

Concerning the launching of their first satellite, they said only that it would come "before the end of the geophysical year"— by the end of 1958.

Several weeks earlier, however, in a guarded interview given only to the Soviet press, Alexander N. Nesmeyanov, head of the Soviet Academy of Science, dropped a hint that the first launching would occur "within the next few months."

But generally Soviet scientists consistently refused to boast about their project or to give the public or other scientists much information about their progress. Key essentials concerning the design of their satellites, their planned altitude, speed and instruments to be carried in the small sphere, were carefully guarded secrets.

CHRONOLOGY

1940

Franklin D. Roosevelt is elected to an unprecedented third term as U.S. president; Winston Churchill becomes Britain's prime minister; Adolf Hitler captures western Europe but fails to conquer Great Britain; United States turns back nine hundred Jews fleeing Nazi persecution on the ocean liner *St. Louis;* the concentration camp at Auschwitz is established; American author John Steinbeck's *The Grapes of Wrath* receives the Pulitzer Prize for fiction.

1941

The Manhattan Project marks the beginning of U.S. atomic weapon development; Japan bombs Pearl Harbor on December 7, forcing the United States into World War II; Roosevelt signs the Lend-Lease Act, which empowers the president to sell, lease, or lend defense materials to nations whose defense is considered important to U.S. security; John Crowe Ransom's *The New Criticism* launches a literary movement by the same name.

1942

Military auxiliaries are created for women in the United States; the War Department encourages industrial organizations to hire women to perform work abandoned by men now serving in the war effort; *Handbook of Federal Indian Law* is published by the Department of the Interior as the first official document concerning Native American law in more than one hundred years; the Grand Coulee Dam, one of the world's largest concrete dams, is completed in Washington; in June, the Congress of Racial Equality (CORE) is formed as a resource for nonviolent demonstrators and civil rights leaders; researchers in the United States develop the first electronic computer.

1942–1943

Soviet victory at Stalingrad forces Nazi Germany to retreat, weakening the German military position.

1942-1946
Japanese Americans are forced into internment camps.

1943
Blues legend Muddy Waters moves from Clarksdale, Mississippi, to Chicago, Illinois, where his music will further evolve to become "urban blues"; Italian dictator Benito Mussolini is deposed; French oceanographer Jacques-Yves Cousteau patents the Aqualung; on May 16, Polish Jews attempt an uprising in the Warsaw Ghetto, and seventy thousand are killed; on June 20, a major race riot breaks out in Detroit's Belle Isle Park.

1944
Allied troops storm the beaches of Normandy on June 6; National Congress of American Indians founded; "GI Bill of Rights" is enacted, providing generous educational benefits to war veterans; American author Alice Walker is born; Austrian American biochemist Erwin Chargaff discovers the genetic function of DNA.

1945
Roosevelt, Stalin, and Churchill meet for the Yalta Conference; Roosevelt's death promotes Vice President Harry S. Truman to the presidency; Allied forces defeat Italy, Germany, and Japan (the last with the atomic bombings of Hiroshima and Nagasaki); concentration camps in Germany are liberated; Ho Chi Minh declares Vietnam's independence; Truman signs the War Brides Act, allowing American soldiers to return home with wives from war zones; Anne Frank dies of typhoid at Bergen-Belsen; American chemist Linus Pauling discovers the cause of sickle-cell anemia; the first atomic bomb is detonated in the desert near Alamogordo, New Mexico.

1946
The "baby boom" begins; the Nuremberg trials hold top Nazi officials accountable for war crimes; the Philippines become independent from the United States after nearly fifty years; the First Indochina War erupts.

1947
India overcomes British rule; the continent is divided into India

and Pakistan; in the United States, Jackie Robinson becomes the first African American professional baseball player; the Truman Doctrine establishes the policy of containment; Anne Frank's diary is published; Indian author Salman Rushdie is born; American author Stephen King is born; American author, poet, and critic Robert Penn Warren's *All the King's Men* receives the Pulitzer Prize for fiction.

1948
Declaration of Human Rights is adopted by the United Nations; President Truman desegregates the American military; Luis Muñoz Marín makes history as Puerto Rico's first elected governor; Gandhi is assassinated; American poet T.S. Eliot receives the Nobel Prize in literature; American playwright Tennessee Williams's *A Streetcar Named Desire* receives the Pulitzer Prize for drama.

1949
The People's Republic of China is established; on September 23, President Truman announces that Russia has test-detonated its first atomic bomb, shifting the balance of atomic power on the world scale; American author William Faulkner receives the Nobel Prize in literature; American playwright Arthur Miller's *Death of a Salesman* receives the Pulitzer Prize for drama.

1950
Senator Joseph McCarthy begins accusations against alleged Communists; Theater of the Absurd characterizes much European and American drama (1950s and early 1960s); on November 2, two members of Puerto Rico's Nationalist Party attempt to assassinate President Truman.

1950–1953
The Korean War wages between North and South Korea.

1951
Julius and Ethel Rosenberg are found guilty of spying for the Soviet Union (they are executed in 1953); the Twenty-Second Amendment is ratified, limiting presidents to two terms in office; color television enters the American market; Libya gains its independence.

1952

American scientist Jonas Salk successfully develops a polio vaccine; Queen Elizabeth II ascends the British throne; Asian American author Amy Tan is born; German philosopher, musicologist, and missionary Albert Schweitzer receives the Nobel Peace Prize.

1953

Stalin dies; Francis Crick and James Watson complete the breakthrough Watson-Crick model of DNA structure; prehistoric drawings are discovered in a cave in France; Sir Winston Churchill receives the Nobel Prize in literature; Piltdown Man, a critical piece of evidence in evolutionary theory is revealed as a fraud; Sir Edmund Hillary leads the first team ever to reach the top of Mount Everest; American author Ernest Hemingway's *The Old Man and the Sea* receives the Pulitzer Prize for fiction.

1954

U.S. Supreme Court strikes down school segregation in *Brown v. Board of Education*; American author Ernest Hemingway receives the Nobel Prize in literature.

1955

The American Federation of Labor (AFL) and the Congress of Industrial Organizations (CIO) merge; Rosa Parks is arrested after refusing to give up her bus seat to a white man; Elvis Presley signs a contract with RCA Records; William F. Buckley Jr. founds the conservative newsmagazine *National Review*; American playwright Tennessee Williams's *Cat on a Hot Tin Roof* receives the Pulitzer Prize for drama.

1956

Anti-Communists in Hungary stage an unsuccessful coup against the Soviet Union's Communist leadership in the country; Dalip Singh Saund is elected to the U.S. House of Representatives, becoming the first Asian American to serve in Congress.

1957

The Soviet Union launches *Sputnik*; in *Roth v. United States* the Supreme Court declares that the First Amendment does not protect obscenity; President Eisenhower sends federal troops to enforce the desegregation of Central High School in Little Rock, Arkansas; Ghana gains its independence.

1958
Alaska becomes a state.

1959
Hawaii becomes a state; Fidel Castro and his rebels take power in Cuba; on July 8, the first two Americans are killed in what will escalate to become the Vietnam War; General Charles de Gaulle becomes France's president.

FOR FURTHER RESEARCH

Books

Barbara Belford, *Brilliant Bylines: A Biographical Anthology of Notable Newspaperwomen in America.* New York: Columbia University Press, 1986.

Victor H. Bernstein, *Final Judgment: The Story of Nuremberg.* New York: Boni & Gaer, 1947.

William J. Bosch, *Judgment on Nuremberg: American Attitudes Toward the Major German War-Crime Trials.* Chapel Hill: University of North Carolina Press, 1970.

Lewis Broad, *Winston Churchill: A Biography.* New York: Hawthorn Books, 1958.

Winston S. Churchill, *Victory: War Speeches by the Right Honorable Winston S. Churchill.* Comp. Charles Eade. Boston: Little, Brown, 1946.

Dictionary of American Biography. Supplement 9. *1971–1975.* New York: Charles Scribner's Sons, 1994.

Dictionary of American History. New York: Charles Scribner's Sons, 1976.

Abraham J. Edelheit and Hershel Edelheit, *History of the Holocaust: A Handbook and Dictionary.* Boulder, CO: Westview, 1994.

Encyclopedia of the Holocaust. New York: Macmillan Reference USA, 1990.

Martin Evans and Ken Lunn, eds., *War and Memory in the Twentieth Century.* Oxford, England: Berg, 1997.

Susanne Everett, Peter Young, and Robin Sommer, *Wars of the Twentieth Century: World War I, World War II, the Korean War, the Vietnam War, the Middle East War.* London: Bison Books, 1985.

Konnilyn G. Feig, *Hitler's Death Camps: The Sanity of Madness.* New York: Homes & Meier, 1981.

Philip S. Foner and Daniel Rosenberg, eds., *Racism, Dissent, and Asian Americans from 1850 to the Present: A Documentary History.* Westport, CT: Greenwood, 1993.

Anne Frank, *The Diary of a Young Girl: The Definitive Edition.* New York: Doubleday, 1995.

Harry A. Gailey, *The War in the Pacific: From Pearl Harbor to Tokyo Bay.* Novato, CA: Presidio, 1997.

Martin Gilbert, *Churchill: A Life.* New York: Holt, 1991.

David Halberstam, *The Fifties.* New York: Fawcett Columbine, 1993.

Patsy Guy Hammontree, *Elvis Presley: A Bio-Bibliography.* Westport, CT: Greenwood, 1985.

William Harmon and C. Hugh Holman, *A Handbook to Literature.* 7th ed. Upper Saddle River, NJ: Prentice-Hall, 1996.

Laura Hein and Mark Selden, eds., *Living with the Bomb: American and Japanese Cultural Conflicts in the Nuclear Age.* New York: M.E. Sharpe, 1997.

Lynn Boyd Hinds and Theodore Otto Windt Jr., *The Cold War as Rhetoric: The Beginnings, 1945–1950.* Westport, CT: Praeger, 1991.

Ted Hipple, ed., *Writers for Young Adults.* New York: Charles Scribner's Sons, 1997.

Steven James Lambakis, *Winston Churchill, Architect of Peace: A Study of Statesmanship and the Cold War.* Ed. Colin Gray. Westport, CT: Greenwood, 1993.

Alan J. Levine, *From the Normandy Beaches to the Baltic Sea: The Northwest Europe Campaign, 1944–1945.* Westport, CT: Praeger, 2000.

———, *The Missile and Space Race.* Westport, CT: Praeger, 1994.

John D. McKenzie, *On Time, on Target: The World War II Mem-*

oir of a Paratrooper in the Eighty-Second Airborne. Novato, CA: Presidio, 2000.

Martin J. Medhurst, *Eisenhower's War of Words: Rhetoric and Leadership.* East Lansing: Michigan State University Press, 1994.

Theodor Meron, *War Crimes Law Comes of Age: Essays.* Oxford, England: University of Oxford, 1998.

Gary Y. Okihiro, *Whispered Silences: Japanese Americans and World War II.* Seattle: University of Washington Press, 1996.

Halford R. Ryan, *Franklin D. Roosevelt's Rhetorical Presidency.* New York: Greenwood, 1988.

John E. Schrecker, *The Chinese Revolution in Historical Perspective.* Westport, CT: Praeger, 1991.

Matthew J. Von Bencke, *The Politics of Space: A History of U.S.-Soviet/Russian Competition and Cooperation in Space.* Boulder, CO: Westview, 1997.

Samuel Walker, *Prompt and Utter Destruction: Truman and the Use of Atomic Bombs Against Japan.* Chapel Hill: University of North Carolina Press, 1997.

Emmy E. Werner, *Through the Eyes of Innocents: Children Witness World War II.* Boulder, CO: Westview, 2000.

B.D. Zevin, ed., *Nothing to Fear: The Selected Addresses of Franklin Delano Roosevelt, 1932–1945.* Boston: Houghton Mifflin, 1946.

Periodicals

Laura Hein, "Remembering the Bomb: The Fiftieth Anniversary in the United States and Japan," *Bulletin of Concerned Asian Scholars,* vol. 27, no. 2, 1995.

Marguerite Higgins, "Thirty-Three Thousand Dachau Captives Freed by Seventh Army," *New York Herald Tribune,* May 1, 1945.

New York Times, "Soviet Fires Earth Satellite into Space," October 5, 1957.

Rinjiro Sodei, "Hiroshima/Nagasaki as History and Politics," *Bulletin of Concerned Asian Scholars*, vol. 27, no. 2, 1995.

Flint Whitlock, "Liberating Dachau," *World War II,* vol. 14, no. 7, March 2000.

Electronic Resources

American Decades CD-ROM. Farmington Hills, MI: Gale Research, 1998.

DISCovering U.S. History. Farmington Hills, MI: Gale Research, 1997.

DISCovering World History. Farmington Hills, MI: Gale Research, 1997.

INDEX